GREAT SPORTS TEAMS

THE SAN ANTONIO SPURS

CHUCK BEDNAR

T 25372

LUCENT
BOOKS®

THOMSON

———— ✳ ———— ™

GALE

San Diego • Detroit • New York • San Francisco • Cleveland
New Haven, Conn. • Waterville, Maine • London • Munich

Produced by OTTN Publishing, Stockton, N.J.

© 2004 by Lucent Books. Lucent Books is an imprint of The Gale Group, Inc., a division of Thomson Learning, Inc.

Lucent Books® and Thomson Learning™ are trademarks used herein under license.

For more information, contact
Lucent Books
27500 Drake Rd.
Farmington Hills, MI 48331-3535
Or you can visit our Internet site at http://www.gale.com

LIBRARY OF CONGRESS CATALOGING-IN-PUBLICATION DATA

Bednar, Chuck, 1976-
  The San Antonio Spurs / by Chuck Bednar.
    p. cm. — (Great sports teams)
  Summary: Discusses the basketball team originally known as the Dallas Chaparrals, which became the San Antonio Spurs in 1973, noting the contributions of such players as James Silas, Johnny Moore, and Tim Duncan.
  Includes bibliographical references and index.
  ISBN 1-59018-242-1 (hardback : alk. paper)
  1. San Antonio Spurs (Basketball team)—Biography—Juvenile literature. 2. Basketball players—United States—Biography—Juvenile literature. [1. San Antonio Spurs (Basketball team) 2. Basketball players.] I. Title. II. Series.
  GV885.52.S26B43 2004
  796.323'64'09764351—dc22

                                    2003014863

Contents

FOREWORD

Former Supreme Court Chief Justice Warren Burger once said he always read the sports section of the newspaper first because it was about humanity's successes, while the front page listed only humanity's failures. Millions of people across the country today would probably agree with Burger's preference for tales of human endurance, record-breaking performances, and feats of athletic prowess. Although these accomplishments are far beyond what most Americans can ever hope to achieve, average people, the fans, do want to affect what happens on the field of play. Thus, their role becomes one of encouragement. They cheer for their favorite players and team and boo the opposition.

ABC Sports president Roone Arledge once attempted to explain the relationship between fan and team. Sport, said Arledge, is "a set of created circumstances—artificial circumstances—set up to frustrate a man in pursuit of a goal. He has to have certain skills to overcome those obstacles—or even to challenge them. And people who don't have those skills cheer him and admire him." Over a period of time, the admirers may develop a rabid—even irrational—allegiance to a particular team. Indeed, the word "fan" itself is derived from the word "fanatic," someone possessed by an excessive and irrational zeal. Sometimes this devotion to a team is because of a favorite player; often it's because of where a person lives, and, occasionally, it's because of a family allegiance to a particular club.

4

Whatever the reason, the bond formed between team and fan often defies reason. It may be easy to understand the appeal of the New York Yankees, a team that has gone to the World Series an incredible thirty-eight times and won twenty-six championships, nearly three times as many as any other major league baseball team. It is more difficult, though, to comprehend the fanaticism of Chicago Cubs fans, who faithfully follow the progress of a team that hasn't won a World Series since 1908. Regardless, the Cubs have surpassed the 2 million mark in home attendance in fourteen of the last seventeen years. In fact, their two highest totals were posted in 1999 and 2000, when the team finished in last place.

Each volume in Lucent's Great Sports Teams in History series examines a team that has left its mark on the "American sports consciousness." Each book looks at the history and tradition of the club in an attempt to understand its appeal and the loyalty—even passion—of its fans. Each volume also examines the lives and careers of people who played significant roles in the team's history. Players, managers, coaches, and front-office executives are represented.

Endnoted quotations help bring the text in each book to life. In addition, all books include an annotated bibliography and a For Further Reading list to supply students with sources for conducting additional individual research.

No one volume can hope to explain fully the mystique of the New York Yankees, Boston Celtics, Dallas Cowboys, or Montreal Canadiens. The Lucent Great Sports Teams in History series, however, gives interested readers a solid start on the road to understanding the mysterious bond that exists between modern professional sports teams and their devoted followers.

The Successful Spurs

The city of San Antonio has a rich, illustrious past. Since the seventeenth century, the flags of six different countries have flown over the area. Today, San Antonio is one of the ten largest U.S. cities, with a population of more than 1.1 million.

Professional basketball in San Antonio has a relatively brief history, but one that is filled with highlights. The Dallas Chaparrals franchise in the American Basketball Association was losing money because fans were not coming to see the team play. In 1973 the team's owners made a unique deal with a San Antonio organization called Professional Sports, Inc. Professional Sports, which agreed to rent the Chaparrals for up to three years, would relocate the franchise to San Antonio. If the basketball team proved to be a financial success there, then Professional Sports would have the option to purchase it at a later date. But if Professional Sports was unhappy with the team's performance at the gate, then the team would return to Dallas and ownership would revert to the original group.

This arrangement worked out well for everyone concerned. The team moved to San Antonio, was renamed the Spurs, and soon began winning both games and die-hard fans. Since arriv-

San Antonio coach Gregg Popovich talks with guards Tony Parker and
Steve Smith. Under Popovich the Spurs won NBA titles in 1999 and 2003.

ing in the city for the 1973–1974 season, the San Antonio Spurs
have won thirteen division championships and two NBA
championships. Spurs stars David Robinson and Tim Duncan
have been chosen as the league's Most Valuable Player, and
dozens of other San Antonio players have appeared in the
NBA's annual All-Star games.

During the 2002–2003 season, the Spurs wrote a brilliant new
chapter in the history of San Antonio basketball. The club finished the regular season with a division-winning 60-22 record;
rolled past conference foes Phoenix, Los Angeles, and Dallas;
and beat the New Jersey Nets in the NBA Finals. The team's
second NBA championship was another exciting moment in
the history of one of the best teams in all of basketball.

CHAPTER 1

The Many Faces of Spurs Basketball

Spurs basketball has taken on many faces over the years. It has been the late-game heroics of James Silas. It has been the overwhelming scoring prowess of George Gervin and the rugged defensive play of Alvin Robertson. It has been the dedication and perseverance of David Robinson. It has been the low-post dominance of the "Twin Towers," Robinson and Tim Duncan. And, since 1973, it has been the unwavering and enthusiastic support of the city of San Antonio.

An ABA Team Is Born

On February 2, 1967, the team now known as the San Antonio Spurs came into existence—only the franchise was not called the Spurs at the time, nor was it located in San Antonio. The club was originally known as the Dallas Chaparrals. The American Basketball Association (ABA) granted the franchise to an investment group for $30,000. But before the team had even played a game, it was sold to another group whose six members combined were worth an estimated $750 million. Despite their considerable financial means, the new owners had little success signing their top draft choices, losing such stars as

8

Nate Archibald, Bill Walton, and JoJo White to the National Basketball Association (NBA). Nonetheless, the Chaparrals initially enjoyed a degree of success in the ABA. During the league's first season, 1967–1968, Dallas finished with a 46-32 record, good for second place in the Western Conference. The team downed the Houston Mavericks in the first round of the playoffs that season, but fell to the New Orleans Buccaneers, four games to one, in the Western Conference Finals. Player-coach Cliff Hagan, a former NBA All-Star, led the way for the Chaps (as the team was nicknamed), averaging 18.2 points per game during that inaugural season.

The next several seasons proved difficult for the Chaparrals. During the 1968–1969 season, Dallas went 41-37 and slipped to fourth in the Western Conference. Attendance also plummeted, falling from 3,200 fans per game during the first season to fewer than 2,900 per game in the second. Attendance continued to decline in the team's third year, despite the fact that the Chaparrals won forty-five games during the 1969–1970 campaign. Basketball in Dallas simply was not working. "The Chaps were one of the better teams in the league," claims author Richard Rambeck, "but the residents of Dallas didn't seem

Attendance is sparse at this game in Dallas between the host Chaparrals and the Denver Rockets during the ABA's initial season, 1967–1968.

to notice. Sometimes fewer than 500 people attended the club's home games."[1]

A Team Without a Home

Desperate to increase the club's fan base, the Chaparrals' owners decided to take drastic action. They changed the team's name to the Texas Chaparrals and decided to play home games at three different locales in the Lone Star State—Dallas, Fort Worth, and Lubbock. This move failed miserably. The team finished 30-54 and was swept in the first round of the playoffs by Utah. Attendance fell once again in Dallas, while numbers in the other two cities were utterly pathetic. A source close to the team later remarked, "We couldn't have done more damage if we had set out to deliberately sabotage the franchise."[2] The team moved back to Dallas full-time in 1971, but it would not remain there for long.

Prior to the 1971–1972 season, the Dallas Chaparrals hired former Milwaukee Bucks assistant Tom Nissalke to coach the team. Nissalke replaced general manager Max Williams, who had been serving as coach since the team dismissed Hagan in January of 1970. Under Nissalke, the team improved to 42-42, which was good enough for third place in the Western Conference. Nissalke earned ABA Coach of the Year honors that season, but the Chaparrals were once again swept by Utah in the first round of the playoffs.

Fan support had reached an all-time low, and the owners were losing patience. As the 1972–1973 season got under way, it was clear that they wanted out. With rumors of a sale swirling, Nissalke left to coach in the NBA. Despite the signing of James Silas, who won ABA Rookie of the Year honors that season, the team sputtered under new coach Babe McCarthy. Dallas finished fifth in the Western Conference with a 28-56 record, missing the playoffs for the first time in franchise history.

In desperation, the ownership group made a unique deal with Professional Sports, Inc., a group of thirty-six San Antonio residents that included Angelo Drossos and B.J. "Red" McCombs. Professional Sports agreed to rent the team for up to three years, relocating it to San Antonio. The Chaps were once again on the move.

James Silas joined the Dallas Chaparrals for the 1972–1973 season, playing well enough to be named the ABA's Rookie of the Year.

San Antonio's Gain

The Dallas Chaparrals were no more, at least for the time being. The team name was supposed to be changed to the San Antonio Gunslingers, but before the start of the 1973–1974 season, another name was chosen instead: the San Antonio Spurs. Nissalke was rehired as head coach.

The team was scheduled to start its first season away from Dallas on October 10, 1973, but the opener was not the storybook beginning the team's new owners wanted. "We had 11,000 tickets to sell, and they told me I still had to fill the place," recalled former Spurs general manager John Begzos. "We could have forced people in with a gun and not filled it. I had to give away tickets."[3]

In the end, about 6,000 people watched the Spurs lose their opener to the San Diego Conquistadors. Begzos recalled the less-than-ideal conditions: "Game time rolled around and there we were, all freezing to death. The building people had set the temperature at 60 degrees. They figured the body heat would warm the place. But with the handful of fans we had, we couldn't have warmed a men's room."[4]

In 1973 the Spurs obtained 6-foot-11 center Swen Nater from the Virginia Squires. Nater was the ABA's Rookie of the Year in 1973–1974.

As the season went on, fans began to warm up to the team. San Antonio played a very slow, deliberate brand of basketball, holding opponents below the 100-point mark an ABA-record forty-nine times. The Spurs also acquired two key players that season—center Swen Nater, who won ABA Rookie of the Year honors in 1973–1974, and George Gervin, who would become one of the greatest players in franchise history. Nater and Gervin combined with Silas to produce a dangerous triple threat. That season, the Spurs finished with a 45-39 record—good enough for third place in the Western Conference.

More important, the team had the support of the people of San Antonio. The largest crowd in team history to that point—more than 12,300 fans—turned out to see an April 10, 1974, playoff game against Indiana. Two other contests in the series, which the Spurs eventually lost in seven games, drew more than 10,000 fans. "The fans were something else," said Begzos. "We came home after a terrible road trip and still drew 6,195 people on New Year's Eve. That would've never happened in Dallas."[5] The team had found a permanent home in San Antonio.

George Gervin joined the Spurs in February 1974 through a controversial deal with the Virginia Squires. He soon became the team's biggest star.

From the ABA to the NBA

Before the 1974–1975 season, the team acquired guard Donnie Freeman from Indiana. Freeman was a big-time scoring threat, and with him, Silas, Nater, and Gervin, big things were expected of the Spurs. The team went undefeated in eight preseason games and won seventeen of its first twenty-seven regular-season contests. However, the Spurs' owners became disenchanted with Nissalke's slow-paced offense and dismissed the coach in the middle of the season. Nissalke's replacement, Bob Bass, promised a more up-tempo playing style. Bass explained his philosophy by saying, "It is my belief that you cannot throw a set offense at another professional team for 48 minutes. You've got to let them play some schoolyard basketball."[6]

The new style was an immediate success, both on and off the court. For example, the Spurs scored 138 points in a January win against St. Louis, and 120 points during a February victory over Denver. San Antonio finished with a 51-33 record, and attendance rose by 25 percent, with an average of nearly 8,000 fans watching every game. But the new coach's approach did not lead to postseason success, as the Indiana Pacers eliminated the Spurs in the first round of the playoffs.

The following season, 1975–1976, San Antonio once again topped the fifty-win mark and finished third in the Western Conference. However, the team was without the injured Silas in the postseason, and the Spurs again bowed out in the first round, losing to New York in seven games.

The 1975–1976 season was the ABA's last. Following the playoffs, the league merged with the more established NBA, and only four ABA teams survived: the New York Nets, the Indiana Pacers, the Denver Nuggets, and the Spurs. In San Antonio, however, Bob Bass did not make the cut—he was replaced as coach by Doug Moe.

The Spurs won their first NBA game, downing the Philadelphia 76ers, 121-118, on October 22, 1976. They finished the season with a 44-38 record, led the league in team scoring with 115 points per game, and reached the playoffs as a number-six seed. Once again, though, the team was ousted in the first round of the playoffs, this time by the Boston Celtics.

Regular-Season Dominance, Playoff Disappointments

Regular-season success, postseason failure—that trend would continue for the Spurs throughout the late 1970s and early 1980s. The Spurs entered the 1977–1978 season with several players out of the lineup with injuries. San Antonio limped to a 16-14 start, but as the team got healthier it began to excel. Finishing the season with everyone but Silas healthy, the Spurs won thirty of their last thirty-nine games to capture first place in the NBA Central Division. It was all for naught, though, as once again the Spurs got bounced in the first round of the playoffs, falling to the Washington Bullets in six games.

San Antonio struggled to a 14-14 start during 1978–1979. But when Silas returned from injuries at midseason, the club regrouped. The clutch-shooting guard teamed with Gervin to lead the Spurs to a 48-34 record and their second consecutive Central Division title. San Antonio proved to be a force in the playoffs as well, rolling past the Philadelphia 76ers and reaching the Eastern Conference Finals. When the Spurs won three of the first four games against Washington, it appeared that they were headed for the NBA Finals at last. But the Bullets roared back to win the last three contests, eliminating San Antonio in a heartbreaking seven-game series.

Gervin once again was San Antonio's dominant player the next season, but the Spurs as a team failed to dominate. During the 1979–1980 campaign, San Antonio struggled on defense, surrendering a league-worst 112.7 points per game. The team's problems would cost Coach Moe his job before the season had ended. After his firing, Bob Bass was brought back. Bass steered San Antonio to a 41-41 finish, good for second place in the Central Division. But once again, the team came up short in the playoffs, falling in the first round.

San Antonio moved to the NBA's Midwest Division before the 1980–1981 season. The Spurs hired a new coach, Stan Albeck, and acquired Dave Corzine from the Bullets and George Johnson as a free agent. Despite the new players, the new division, and the new coach, the results seemed painfully familiar for San Antonio fans. The Spurs rolled to a 52-30 regular-season record and won the Western Conference's Midwest Division before floundering yet again in the playoffs. This year San Antonio bowed to Houston in the conference semifinals.

Following the 1980–1981 season, the Spurs decided to trade James Silas, the last remaining San Antonio player to have played as a Chaparral. The emergence of rookie point guard Johnny Moore had made the veteran Silas expendable.

In his second year, 1981–1982, Moore led the league in assists. Teamed with Gervin, who averaged 32.3 points per game that season, Moore led the Spurs to a second straight Midwest

Division title. San Antonio bounced back from two games down in the first round of the playoffs, winning three straight games to eliminate the Seattle SuperSonics. Although San Antonio reached the Western Conference Finals, they were swept by the Los Angeles Lakers, who went on to win the NBA title.

Before the 1982–1983 season, the Spurs again tinkered with their lineup, trading Corzine to Chicago for eleven-year veteran Artis Gilmore. An intimidating presence at 7-foot-2, the center helped San Antonio finish the regular season with a 53-29 record. The Spurs were dominant in all aspects of the game—as a team San Antonio was second in the NBA in scoring, rebounding, shot blocking, and assists. Gilmore led the league in field-goal percentage (.626), Moore was second in assists (9.8 per game), and Gervin was fourth in scoring (26.5 points per game). The Spurs returned to the postseason and powered past the Denver Nuggets in five games, setting up a second-round rematch with the Lakers. This year San Antonio made a better showing, but the team still could not upend L.A., falling in six games.

The Spurs had won their division five times in six seasons, yet they had failed even to reach the NBA Finals, let alone win a title. Now San Antonio was about to experience lows it had never seen before. Albeck left to coach the Nets before the start of the 1983–1984

In the 1982–1983 season, veteran center Artis Gilmore joined San Antonio, helping the Spurs to their third straight Midwest Division title.

season and was replaced by Morris McHone. The team got out of the gates slowly, struggling to a 6-12 start. Gilmore battled injuries, and Gervin was beginning to slow down at this point in his career. In fact, during one December game, the Iceman (as Gervin was known) was held to under ten points for the first time in 407 consecutive games. McHone did not last through December, and Bass, stepping in to coach the team for the third time, did not fare any better. San Antonio finished with a 37-45 record and failed to make the playoffs for the first time since joining the NBA. Unfortunately for Spurs fans, things were not about to improve anytime soon.

The Downward Spiral Begins

Early in the 1984–1985 season it seemed as if new coach Cotton Fitzsimmons had righted the ship. San Antonio won five of its first six games. Then the bottom fell out: The Spurs lost their next seven in a row and ultimately finished with a .500 record. Reaching the playoffs as the eighth and final seed in the Western Conference, the team battled valiantly, taking the Denver Nuggets to five games before bowing out.

In 1985, desperate to turn the Spurs around, Fitzsimmons traded aging superstar George Gervin to the Chicago Bulls. The move would allow Alvin Robertson, drafted seventh overall by the team the previous year, to move into the starting lineup. Fitzsimmons explained, "The Spurs were always known as a high-scoring offensive team led by Ice, but we needed toughness and quickness. Alvin gave us that look."[7]

Robertson seemed ready to fill the void left by Gervin's departure, claiming, "He's still the main man around here. Nothing will change that. But, honestly, I felt I outplayed him every time in the preseason. Every time."[8] To his credit, Robertson did play well, leading the league in steals and winning the NBA Most Improved Player and NBA Defensive Player of the Year honors. However, after a 19-13 start, the team lost Johnny Moore when the point guard came down with a rare disease called desert fever. The Spurs struggled to a 35-47 record—the club's worst mark in San Antonio to that point.

Although Fitzsimmons was replaced as coach by Bob Weiss for the 1986–1987 season, the team's fortunes did not improve.

As the Spurs struggled, Weiss used seventeen different starters in an attempt to find a successful combination. Nothing worked. Despite a second strong season from Robertson, who repeated as the NBA's Defensive Player of the Year, San Antonio finished with a ghastly mark of 28 wins and 54 losses. But the horrible season may have been the best thing ever to happen to the Spurs. That is because it enabled San Antonio to win the NBA's draft lottery and use the first pick to snag Navy center David Robinson. However, because of Robinson's commitment to serve in the military, he would not be able to join the team for two years.

The Spurs carried on while waiting for the player many felt would finally change the franchise's fortunes. During the 1987–1988 season, the Spurs finished below .500 again, but their 31-51 record was somehow good enough for a playoff berth. San Antonio quickly exited from the postseason, however, as the Lakers swept them in the first round.

Before the 1988–1989 season, Angelo Drossos sold his stake in the Spurs to Red McCombs, and Weiss was replaced by a new coach, Larry Brown. However, injuries and poor play doomed the team to the worst record in franchise history (21-61). Help was on the way, though—the Admiral was ready to report for duty.

The Pieces Come Together

David Robinson joined the Spurs in May 1989. Shortly thereafter, Brown dealt Alvin Robertson and another player for Terry Cummings. The Spurs also added Sean Elliott in the draft, and Maurice Cheeks in a later trade. In all, there were nine new players on the Spurs' roster by opening day. The wheeling and dealing paid off, as San Antonio engineered the biggest turnaround in NBA history, finishing the 1989–1990 campaign with a 56-26 record. Robinson was named Rookie of the Year, and the Spurs reached the Western Conference Semifinals, where they lost a heartbreaking seven-game series to the Portland Trail Blazers.

The Spurs won their second straight Midwest Division crown in 1990–1991, finishing with a 55-27 record. This time, first-round foe Golden State upset San Antonio in four games.

Starting point guard Rod Strickland sat out the early part of the following season because of a contract dispute. Without him the team struggled, and Larry Brown resigned. Bob Bass once again filled in as San Antonio's coach, guiding the team to a 47-35 record. However, the Spurs lost Robinson for the playoffs when the Admiral underwent surgery to repair a torn ligament in his hand. Once again San Antonio suffered an opening-round playoff sweep, this time at the hands of the Phoenix Suns.

The Spurs hired a big-name college coach, Jerry Tarkanian, to direct the team for 1992–1993. Tarkanian proved to be a big-name bust, though, as San Antonio lost four of its first five games. Just a quarter of the way through the season, Tarkanian called it quits, stepping down with his team holding a lackluster

After David Robinson joined the Spurs for the 1989–1990 season, San Antonio won thirty-five more games than it had in the previous season.

9-11 record. He replacement was John Lucas, a former Spurs guard. Also during the season, McCombs sold his stake in the team to a group of twelve investors. With Lucas at the helm and the new ownership in place, San Antonio surged to finish with a 49-33 record. Once again, though, the team sputtered in the playoffs and was eventually eliminated by the Suns.

San Antonio's trend of playoff frustration continued over the next several seasons. Despite acquiring the rebound-happy Dennis Rodman in the off-season—a move that helped Robinson win the 1993–1994 scoring title—the Spurs failed to make it past the first round of the playoffs. After the season Lucas was replaced by Bob Hill and Rodman was traded.

During the next two years under Hill, the Spurs won back-to-back Midwest Division crowns and were victorious in 121 of 164 regular-season games. Robinson won the 1994–1995 MVP Award. Still, the Spurs did not reach the NBA championship series, losing in the Western Conference Finals in 1994–1995 and falling to the Utah Jazz in the second round of the 1995–1996 playoffs.

On the face of it the 1996–1997 campaign was an utter disaster. En route to an abysmal 20-62 record, the Spurs made yet another coaching change, replacing Hill with Gregg Popovich. But, as had happened ten years earlier, the team's failure laid the groundwork for successes to come: After the season San Antonio won the NBA draft lottery for the second time in franchise history. Once again the Spurs chose wisely, spending the number-one pick on forward/center Tim Duncan of Wake Forest University.

Duncan paid immediate dividends, teaming with Robinson to help San Antonio win 56 games during the 1997–1998 season. The Spurs had the look of a possible title contender, but they were unable to get past the Utah Jazz in the Western Conference Semifinals.

Still, Robinson and Duncan were a formidable combination during their first year together. Both were All-Stars, and both were among the league leaders in scoring, rebounding, blocks, and double-doubles (games in which a player tallies ten or more in two major statistical categories, such as points, rebounds, assists, steals, or blocked shots). Duncan averaged 21.1

Tim Duncan blocks a shot against the backboard glass. After Duncan joined the Spurs in 1997, he helped San Antonio win a pair of NBA titles.

points and 11.9 rebounds per game while leading the NBA with 57 double-doubles. Robinson, meanwhile, averaged 21.6 points and 10.6 rebounds per game. The duo also combined to block an average of 5.14 shots per game. These were impressive statistics by any standard, and the best was yet to come.

Reaching the Pinnacle

Spurs fans had been growing impatient. The team had been in existence since 1967 but had never claimed a championship in either the ABA or the NBA. As the lockout-shortened 1998–1999 season started, and the club struggled to a 6-8 record in February, the fans lashed out. "Many fans," writer Gene Hoffman observed, "were calling for the axing of head coach Gregg Popovich and the trading of David Robinson, who had sacrificed a great deal of his offensive output to Tim Duncan."[9] However, fan unrest turned to cheers as the Spurs turned their season around, winning 31 of their remaining 36 games to finish with the NBA's best record.

San Antonio's dominance continued throughout the playoffs. The Spurs needed just five games to bounce Kevin Garnett and the Minnesota Timberwolves in the first round. They then kicked into high gear, sweeping Shaquille O'Neal, Kobe Bryant, and the Los Angeles Lakers in the second round. The Spurs also swept the Portland Trail Blazers in the Western Conference Finals, thanks in part to an amazing shot by Sean Elliott at the end of game two that has since been dubbed the "Memorial Day Miracle." At last, after twenty-six years, the Spurs were headed to the NBA Finals.

Duncan and the Spurs went right to work against their opponents, the New York Knicks. The Wake Forest grad scored 33 points and snagged 16 rebounds to lead San Antonio to an 89-77 victory in the series opener. San Antonio won two of the next three games to take a commanding lead in the series. In game five the Spurs trailed 77-76 with less than a minute to play. That's when Elliot, guarded fiercely by New York's Latrell Sprewell, found Avery Johnson open. Johnson lofted an eighteen-foot jumper, burying what would become the game-winner. The San Antonio Spurs were NBA champions.

Although Duncan was named series MVP, most observers credited the Spurs' suffocating defense for the victory. San Antonio set playoff records by holding New York to the fewest points, fewest field goals, and fewest assists by a team over a five-game series. The Spurs limited the Knicks to an average of 79.8 points per game during the Finals. "We preached defense all year and that defense wins championships," the Spurs' Antonio Daniels said after the fifth game. "That's what Spurs basketball was all about this year."[10]

Hard Road to a Second Title

Unfortunately for San Antonio fans, the next few years would bring more regular-season success and playoff disappointment for the Spurs. In 1999–2000, the team finished with fifty-three wins but was bumped from the playoffs in the first round by the Phoenix Suns. San Antonio posted identical 58-24 records and captured division titles in both 2000–2001 and 2001–2002, but each season ended with a disappointing playoff loss to the Los Angeles Lakers.

In 2002–2003, the Spurs finished the regular season with a 60-22 record, good for their thirteenth division championship. In the postseason, the Spurs defeated the Phoenix Suns in the first round, setting up a third consecutive showdown with Los Angeles, which had won three straight NBA titles. This time, the Spurs prevailed over the Lakers in six games. Then San Antonio outlasted the Dallas Mavericks, a team that had also won sixty regular-season games, in the Western Conference Finals.

In San Antonio's second trip to the championship series, the team would face the New Jersey Nets. This marked the first time in NBA history that two former ABA franchises had met in the NBA Finals. The last time the Nets and Spurs had faced each other in the playoffs was in 1976, during the ABA's final season. At that time, Julius Erving and the Nets had handed the Spurs a first-round playoff loss in a seven-game series.

The first four games of the 2003 NBA Finals were closely contested. San Antonio opened the series with a 101-89 victory, but New Jersey held off a late Spurs rally for an 87-85 win in the second game. The Spurs struggled early in game three, but so did the Nets. After the lowest-scoring first half in NBA Finals history, Duncan and Tony Parker took control, combining for forty-seven points in an 84-79 San Antonio victory.

The momentum shifted back to New Jersey in game four. Although San Antonio shot just 29.8 percent from the field (the third-worst shooting performance in NBA Finals history), the Spurs were still within striking distance until the very end. With seconds remaining, Manu Ginobili managed to shake his defender and launch a three-point attempt that would have sent the game into overtime. It fell short, and New Jersey won the game, 77-76, to tie the series at two games apiece.

Duncan came through in game five, scoring 29 points in San Antonio's 93-83 victory. With their backs against the wall, the Nets came out fighting in the sixth game. Early in the fourth period, San Antonio was trailing by nine points. But then the Spurs started playing like champions. San Antonio went on a 19-0 run, outscoring the Nets 31-14 during the period to secure an 88-77 win and the franchise's second NBA championship.

*San Antonio rookie guard Emanuel "Manu" Ginobili celebrates with the
NBA Championship trophy at the Alamodome, June 2003.*

Duncan finished the sixth game with a triple-double—21
points, 20 rebounds, and 10 assists. He also blocked eight
shots in the game (giving him a series total of 32 blocks, an
NBA Finals record), and he was named MVP of the Finals for
the second time in his career. "I thought this was the most
poise we showed all season long—having the pitfalls we had
in the playoffs then putting the game together we did today,"
he said afterward.[11]

The victory was especially sweet for David Robinson, who
retired at the end of the season. "To finish my career in the
NBA Finals and to win the championship is a play written only
by God," he told AP basketball writer Chris Sheridan.[12] For the
Admiral, who scored 13 points and snagged 17 rebounds in the
decisive game, going out a champion was the ultimate retirement present.

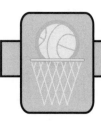

CHAPTER 2

James Silas

Some athletes can take over a game at the crucial moment. James Silas was one of these clutch players. Silas's statistics are not as flashy as those of some other Spurs greats, such as his teammate George Gervin. Silas led San Antonio in scoring only once during his career. Yet the Spurs could always count on "Captain Late" when they needed a fourth-quarter comeback. When the pressure was on, Silas was at his best.

The Unknown Star

James Silas was born in Tallulah, Louisiana, in 1949. He was one of eight children, but the size of the family and other circumstances made it difficult for the Silas clan to spend much time together. It was, as author Nathan Aaseng put it, "a loose-knit family in which everyone often went his or her separate way. One of James' sisters, in fact, never saw him play basketball until he reached the pros."[13]

Silas played basketball at McCall High School, where he had a solid career. But he was overlooked by larger colleges. After graduating from McCall, he enrolled in Stephen F. Austin University, a National Association of Intercollegiate Athletics

(NAIA) school in Nacogdoches, Texas. (The NAIA is a small-college equivalent of the National Collegiate Athletic Association, or NCAA.)

As a collegian, Silas continued to excel. In 1970 and 1971 he was named to both the All Lone Star Conference First Team and the NAIA All American First Team. He averaged 18.7 points per game during his career with the Lumberjacks and set fourteen school records. His finest college season came as a senior, when he averaged 30.7 points per game and led the Lumberjacks to a 29-1 record. Still, Silas's accomplishments went virtually unnoticed by the media and by professional scouts. This was due largely to the fact that he played for a small school that was hardly a traditional basketball power-house. "No one heard of Stephen F. Austin even though we had a good team," Silas once told *Basketball Weekly's* Dan Pattison. "The bigger schools get the ink and television exposure. I thought I was as good as anyone I read about. I always thought I was as good as the big college guards."[14]

Silas (left) defends during a college game. His college accomplishments were sometimes overlooked because Stephen F. Austin was a small school.

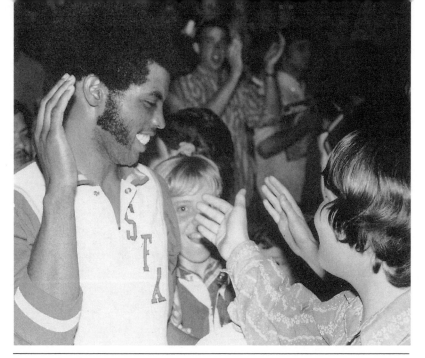

Silas greets young fans after a Stephen F. Austin contest.

After college, Silas was selected in the fourth round of the 1972 draft by the NBA's Houston Rockets. His stay in Houston would be short, however: The Rockets released the young guard before the start of the 1972–1973 season. Silas was furious. "I felt like they knew they were going to cut me all along," he said. "But they waited until before the first regular season game. By that time, most of the rosters were stable. They should've let me go earlier to get on with someone else."[15]

Just as he had feared, Silas cleared NBA waivers. Either no other team in the league wanted him, or they just did not have a roster spot for him.

Silas waited for his chance. Finally, in late November 1972, Dallas Chaparrals coach Babe McCarthy asked Silas to join his ABA club. Silas did not hesitate to take McCarthy up on his offer. He finished the 1972–1973 season as a Chaparral, averaging 13.7 points per game and winning ABA Rookie of the Year honors. For the rising star, it was sweet redemption.

"I'm happy now," the Dallas guard said. "They say to try not to look at the past. I had never been cut by a team. It was humiliating at the time. That's the only regret I have now."[16] Silas was about to make other teams regret not giving him a chance.

James Silas was nicknamed "Captain Late" because of his ability to come through in the clutch and win games for the Spurs.

The Early Days of "Captain Late"

The franchise moved from Dallas to San Antonio following Silas's first year. The next season, 1973–1974, Silas played in every game, increasing his scoring average to 15.7 points per game and averaging 4.1 rebounds and 3.8 assists.

The following year, Silas's production jumped to nearly twenty points and five assists per game. With new teammates George Gervin and Swen Nater, Silas powered San Antonio to fifty-one victories during the 1974–1975 season. At the All-Star Game, he came off the bench to score 21 points.

Silas's numbers were impressive, but not as impressive as his ability to take over late in the game with his team trailing. In fact, he was so good in the clutch that he earned the nickname Captain Late. "When the clock started to wind down in a close game, the Spurs' strategy was to toss the ball to Silas and clear out of the way," claims Aaseng. "James seemed to thrive on pressure like plants thrive on water and sunshine."[17]

Silas would often do most of his scoring in the fourth quarter, at times racking up as many as twenty points in the final period. Spurs coach Bob Bass called Silas "such a good player when the clock was running out that he defied description."[18]

Though Silas had already gained a reputation as a clutch player, 1975–1976 was his breakout year. He again played in every regular-season game, averaging 23.8 points per game and making 52 percent of his field-goal attempts. He also averaged four rebounds and a career-best 5.4 assists per game. In the balloting for the ABA's Most Valuable Player, Silas finished second behind only Julius Erving, who took home his third straight MVP trophy. Regardless, there was no doubting Silas's talent. "He could accelerate, he could explode, he could shoot and he could jump over people," said Bass.[19]

"He really was the best," added Louie Dampier, who played both with and against Silas during his career.[20]

Down but Not Out

Hopes were high for the Spurs as they entered the 1975–1976 NBA playoffs. Then, in the opening game of San Antonio's first-round series against the New York Nets, Silas fell on Brian Taylor and broke his right ankle. Without their leading scorer, the Spurs lost in seven games.

The ABA folded before the next season, and San Antonio was one of four teams absorbed into the NBA. A healthy Silas looked forward to the opportunity. Things would not work out the way he had hoped, though.

During the second quarter of a preseason game against the Kansas City Kings, Silas dodged several opposing players and drove toward the basket. He stopped and launched a shot over

Kansas City forward Bill Robinzine. Silas crashed into Robinzine and went down to the floor. He felt a sharp pain in his left knee but continued to play. The next day he could not run.

Silas, playing despite the injury, scored 18 points in San Antonio's first regular-season NBA game. However, the pain soon became too much. He played in just three of his team's next six games. "I would play a game, then rest, then play," Silas told John Papanek of *Sports Illustrated*. "But the knee felt like something was holding it, like it was locked."[21]

Finally, in November, he decided to undergo surgery to repair the knee. During the procedure, doctors removed dam-

By the time the ABA folded after the 1975–1976 season, Silas had established himself as one of the league's biggest stars.

aged cartilage. Silas missed six weeks rehabilitating his knee. He returned on January 5, 1977, in a game against former ABA rival Denver in which Silas played twenty-eight minutes and scored twenty-eight points. After the game, however, the pain returned. "When I got into the car that night," he recalled, "the knee was so stiff I couldn't bend it. But I figured that I hadn't played in a while and the stiffness would go away. But the next day it was terrible. I couldn't walk."[22]

Silas played in just twenty-two games for the Spurs during the 1976–1977 season and averaged fewer than ten points per game. It was his worst year as a professional player. He was frightened by his condition. "I came back thinking, 'I want to be like I was before I got hurt,'" he said. "I wanted to jump as high, penetrate, do all the things I knew how to do. And this was the first time I had all those things taken away from me. It was scary."[23]

Silas underwent a second knee operation before the 1977–1978 season, but the knee showed no noticeable improvement. "The first day of training camp I felt great," Silas remembered, "but the next morning I couldn't walk again. Now I said, "Hey, I'm through. Jimmy, you're not going to play again!'"[24] Thanks largely to the encouragement of his fellow Spurs, however, Silas stayed with the club.

Another Comeback for Captain Late

During the 1977–1978 season, Silas averaged just eight minutes and four points per game as a reserve while his knee slowly continued to heal. He went to another doctor, who removed bone spurs from the knee and sent Silas back to rehab. When he returned to the team, Silas worked hard, playing one-on-one with center Coby Dietrick, a teammate since his ABA days. The hard work paid off. At one point late in the season, Silas appeared in fourteen straight games—something he had not been able to do since suffering the injury. Still, his playing time was limited.

Meanwhile, his teammates excelled without him. Gervin won the NBA scoring title and San Antonio captured the Central Division with a 52-30 record.

Though depressed about his lack of playing time, Silas was not ready to bring the curtain down on his career. Former coach

Bob Bass phoned him frequently, encouraging him to continue his rehabilitation and convincing him that a comeback was still possible. After the 1977–1978 season ended, Silas worked harder than he had ever worked before. He lifted weights, did leg raises, stretched, and continued honing his skills on the court. He could feel the knee slowly improving, and eventually it had healed to around 75 percent. Silas felt ready for the upcoming season, but he was also worried that if this comeback attempt failed, he might not get another chance.

Silas entered the 1978–1979 season as the Spurs' third guard, behind Gervin and Mike Gale. His first game back was an exhibition contest against Kansas City. Silas was understandably nervous. "Coming back was just like leaving high school and playing your first college game," he said. "The floor looked bigger, the leg felt naked. Every move I made was cautious. I didn't want anything to happen to me."[25] Silas's fears were unwarranted. He scored eighteen points in twenty minutes against the Monarchs.

During the first twenty-eight games of the regular season, Silas came off the bench to average 13 points and 21 minutes per game. The Spurs struggled early in the season, however. By December 15, they finally reached the .500 mark with victories over New York and Indiana. The Spurs were in third place in their division, chasing Atlanta and Houston. Coach Moe decided a lineup change was in order. He put Silas in the starting lineup and sent Gale to the bench. The move worked. "The Spurs began winning in bunches," reported Papanek in *Sports Illustrated*. "Gervin has been scoring in torrents, as usual, but at pressure points, where the Spurs had been coming undone, it was Silas who once again was the agent of control . . . he has regained his leadership."[26]

Silas played in 79 games that season, averaging 16 points and 3.5 assists per game. Captain Late was back.

The Clock Finally Runs Out

Silas continued to play well during the 1979–1980 season. He appeared in 77 games, averaging nearly 18 points and 4.5 assists per game. In three postseason appearances that year, he averaged more than 14 points per game. The following season, Silas again

In January 1977, after missing the first part of the season with a knee injury, Silas returned to score twenty-eight points against the Denver Nuggets.

averaged almost 18 points per game, but his playing time dropped with the emergence of a rookie point guard named Johnny Moore. His assist numbers also dropped, to 3.8 per game.

After the Houston Rockets eliminated the Spurs in the 1981 Western Conference Semifinals, San Antonio's front office decided that changes needed to be made—and Silas, the last of the original Dallas Chaparrals, might have to be moved. During the playoffs, the veteran guard had averaged fewer than twelve points and three assists per game, whereas Moore, playing five fewer minutes per game, had averaged six points and four assists. The rookie also averaged more assists per regular-season game while playing just nineteen minutes per contest.

Captain Late shoots a jumper. In James Silas's ten professional seasons (four ABA, six NBA), he scored 11,038 points and dished out 2,628 assists.

The choice was a difficult one, but in the end San Antonio's owners decided that the team's future lay with Johnny Moore rather than James Silas.

Silas was traded to Cleveland before the beginning of the 1981–1982 season. He played in sixty-seven games for the Cavaliers, but by this time age and his knee injuries had caught up with him. Silas's production plummeted: he averaged just over eleven points per game, and he dished out only forty assists for the entire season. While San Antonio went on to win its second straight Midwest Division title, Cleveland ended the season with a 15-67 record—the worst in the Central Division. Silas decided to call it a career.

An Underrated Star

Silas remained involved with basketball after his professional playing days were over. For several years, he has run a basketball camp in Austin, Texas, and in January 2003 he joined the Texas Ambassadors, a group that sponsors basketball tournaments for children. He and his wife, Vanessa, have a son, Xavier.

Despite his exceptional ten-year career, James Silas fails to command the respect accorded to other Spurs greats. Yet he was the team's first star, and he remains among the franchise's career leaders in games played, points, field goals, field goal attempts, and steals. His jersey number, 13, was the first retired by the San Antonio Spurs.

One reason Silas's successes went unnoticed was that he spent a large part of his career in the ABA. But those who played with him—and those who played against him—recognize how great he was. "He was not only the best in [the ABA]," said former ABA and NBA coach Hubie Brown, "he was one of the two or three best in either league."[27]

Silas will always be remembered for his ability to take over late in the game and lead his team to an improbable victory. This was something he continued to do, even near the end of his career. During a 1981 game against the Milwaukee Bucks, Silas's team trailed 106-105 with just seconds to play. Silas hit a long jump shot and was fouled in the process. The three-point play made it 108-106. Milwaukee came back to tie, then double-teamed Silas to make sure that he could not perform any more last-minute heroics. Yet Silas still managed to split the defenders and sink the game-winning basket as the clock ran out.

Even late in his career, Silas was the go-to guy at the end of the game. He was still, and always will be, Captain Late—the best clutch player most fans have never heard of.

CHAPTER 3

George Gervin

When a basketball legend like Hall of Famer Jerry West refers to someone as "the one player I would pay to see,"[28] it is a compliment of the highest order. And perhaps such praise, which West bestowed during a 1982 interview with the *Los Angeles Times*, sums up the career of the man he was referring to better than any records or statistics ever could. For such was George Gervin's incredible ability to improvise on the basketball court that, like Julius Erving and Michael Jordan, he had to be seen to be believed.

Out of the Ghetto

The man who would reach the heights of basketball greatness began life in difficult circumstances. He was born on April 27, 1952, in an inner-city area of Detroit, Michigan. His family was poor, and to make matters worse, his father abandoned George's mother and her six children when George was just two years old.

George's mother went from job to job attempting to support her children. Despite her efforts, George and his family often had to rely on charity groups just to eat.

George Gervin was one of the greatest scoring threats of his generation. Only two players in NBA history—Wilt Chamberlain and Michael Jordan—won more scoring titles than Gervin's four.

George turned to basketball to escape the horror and despair of ghetto life, using a back-alley court near his cousin's house to hone his skills. "It was a poverty area," he recalled. "There was trash and rats but there was nowhere else to go. . . . I just wanted to play basketball."[29]

During his freshman year at Martin Luther King High School in Detroit, George stood only 5-foot-6 and weighed less than 125 pounds. A janitor at the school befriended George and gave him access to the gymnasium, where he would practice every night. Sometimes, he would take as many as a thousand shots in a single evening. In return, a grateful George would sweep the gym floor. It was not unusual for him to remain alone in the empty gym until midnight, shooting the basketball and sweeping the floor.

"He realized later that his time alone in the gymnasium served two purposes," wrote biographer John McNamara. "First, it gave him a skill, a means of escaping the poverty of the city. Second, it kept him away from the temptations of the street and out of trouble."[30]

During his sophomore year George, now 5-foot-8, decided to try out for his high school team. He failed to make the varsity squad but won a spot on the junior varsity team. Over the next couple of years, his basketball skills grew in tandem with his physical development.

By his senior year, 1968–1969, he stood 6-foot-4 and had blossomed into a star on the varsity team. That season, Gervin averaged 31 points and 20 rebounds per game and took his school to the Michigan state quarterfinals. He was named an All-American and All-State player, and he attracted the attention of a high-powered college coach, Long Beach State's Jerry Tarkanian. Upon graduation from Martin Luther King High, Gervin accepted a scholarship to play for Tarkanian.

Risking It All

Although Long Beach State was a basketball power, Gervin quickly discovered that he was unhappy at the school. Homesick and uncomfortable with the culture of Southern California, he dropped out even before the 1969–1970 season had begun. After returning to Detroit, Gervin transferred to Eastern Michigan University in nearby Ypsilanti.

Playing forward for the Eagles as a sophomore, Gervin averaged 29.5 points per game during the 1971–1972 season. At one point during that season he led Eastern Michigan to eighteen straight wins. Though Gervin was becoming a basketball sensation, one fit of anger nearly cost him everything.

The incident took place during a Division II playoff game against Roanoke College. With Eastern Michigan down by fifteen points late in the game, Gervin elbowed Roanoke's Jay Piccola as the two went for a rebound. After a referee ejected him from the game, Gervin calmly walked over to Piccola, as if to apologize for the foul. Instead, he threw a vicious punch that knocked the Roanoke player to the court. "I was just so frustrated and my frustration flared up and I hit the guy," Gervin later recalled. "I can't explain it any better than that. And I tell you: either on a court or off it, that was my only fight."[31]

The backlash from the incident was swift. Eagles coach Jim Dutcher was forced to resign. Gervin was suspended immediately for the following season, and he was later kicked off the

team for good. Invitations to
play in the Olympics and the
Pan Am Games were with-
drawn. Suddenly, George
Gervin was a man without a
team and, seemingly, without a
future. "He was in tears,"
Gervin's high school coach,
Willie Merriweather, remembered. "He didn't know what to
do or where to go."[32]

With few other options,
Gervin signed a contract with
the Pontiac Chaparrals, a mi-
nor-league team in the Eastern
Basketball Association. The contract paid only about $500 per
month, but it was enough for
Gervin. "I was down," he said,
"but I had an apartment, a car,
and I was making money doing
what I loved most."[33]

*Gervin was a fluid scorer,
known for his finger-roll shots,
pictured here.*

Gervin also had luck on his
side. A scout for the American
Basketball Association's Virginia Squires happened to be in
the crowd during a 1972 game when Gervin exploded for fifty
points. The scout offered him a tryout, and Gervin took full ad-
vantage, impressing the Squires' coaches. Soon he was signing
a deal with the club worth $100,000 per season. His basketball
career, which seemed all but dead after the Roanoke incident,
had been given new life.

The Sale of George Gervin

Gervin joined Virginia midway through the 1972–1973 season.
Teammate Fatty Taylor initially dubbed him "Iceberg Slim" because of his slender build, but that nickname would not last
long. Once his teammates saw his cool composure on the court,
the nickname was altered to "the Iceman." During his first sea-

son with the Squires, Gervin averaged 14.1 points per game. Another teammate, future Hall of Famer Julius Erving, won the ABA scoring title that season by averaging 31.9 points per game.

Virginia was a talented team, but it was in serious financial trouble. Owner Earl Foreman began selling some of the Squires' best players—including such greats as Rick Barry, Dave Bing, and Bob McAdoo—to other ABA clubs. Foreman also did business with Spurs owner Angelo Drossos, selling him the contract of center Swen Nater in November 1973.

While his teammates were being auctioned off around him, Gervin played some of the best basketball of his life during the first half of the 1973–1974 season. He ranked among the ABA's top five scorers and was selected to the league's All-Star Game. The day of the All-Star Game, his contract was sold to San Antonio for $225,000. According to *San Antonio Express-News* reporter David King, "Foreman was looking to sell the team, but wanted what he could get for the players first."[34]

Mike Storen, the ABA's commissioner, had seen enough of the Virginia franchise's fire sale. Storen pressured Foreman to rescind the Gervin deal, arguing that getting rid of the team's best players would make the club harder to sell. Gervin was not thrilled about being shipped out either—he did not want to leave teammates Erving and Taylor behind. The deal authorizing the sale was signed on January 13, 1974, but before the end of the month, Foreman changed his mind and attempted to nullify the transaction.

Drossos filed a lawsuit in a federal court in San Antonio, arguing that the purchase of Gervin's contract was legally binding and had to be enforced. Storen attempted to placate Drossos, offering the owner a full refund plus interest, attorneys' fees, and the rights to Virginia player George Carter in exchange for Gervin's return to the Squires. Drossos agreed. However, while Storen was negotiating with Drossos, Foreman sold the Virginia franchise to a group of investors. The team's new owners balked at the deal and demanded Gervin's return without compensation. Ultimately, Storen yielded to their demands and announced that the league would not permit the sale of George Gervin. Drossos, insisting that Storen did not have that authority, went forward with legal action.

On February 6, Adrian Spears, the judge handling the case, issued a ten-day injunction that temporarily made the Iceman a Spur. Gervin reported to San Antonio the next day and began playing for the Spurs. During the week of February 11, the hearing commenced. Following several days of testimony from Drossos, Storen, San Antonio coach Tom Nissalke, and others, Judge Spears granted a second temporary injunction in favor of the Spurs. On March 3, the judge ruled in favor of Drossos, deciding that Storen did not have the authority to cancel a valid transaction and that the sale of Gervin's contract to the Spurs was legally binding.

As a result, Gervin finished the 1973–1974 season with the Spurs. He averaged 23.4 points per game, fourth best in the ABA. Though he had been reluctant to leave Virginia, it did not take him long to warm up to the city of San Antonio. "Once I got here and saw how the fans were, the love they had for their basketball team, I knew I had found a home," Gervin said.[35] And, as Spurs fans quickly discovered, the team had found a player who would become the cornerstone of the franchise's success for years to come.

The Iceman Cometh . . . to the NBA

In each of the next two seasons, Gervin was named an All-Star and finished in the top ten in scoring. During the 1974–1975 season he played in all eighty-four games, averaging 23.4 points, 8.3 rebounds, and 2.5 assists per game. The following year, in what would be his final season in the ABA, he averaged 21.8 points, 6.7 rebounds, and 2.5 assists in eighty-one games played.

When the ABA folded and the Spurs joined the NBA, many people expected Gervin to have a much rougher road in the more established league. They were wrong. The Iceman averaged more than twenty-three points per game during the 1976–1977 campaign, then confirmed his greatness the following season in a classic battle for the NBA scoring title.

During the 1977–1978 season, Gervin powered San Antonio to the Central Division title. Going into the final day of the season, he was locked in a dogfight with David Thompson of the Denver Nuggets for the NBA scoring title. The Nuggets' last game of the season was an afternoon matchup against Detroit, and in the first quarter Thompson broke Wilt Chamberlain's record for most points in a quarter by sinking thirty-two. The Denver star wound up with an amazing seventy-three points, at the time the third-highest single-game total ever. "I guess

Though Gervin had starred in the ABA, many people questioned whether he would stand out in the more established NBA. He proved his doubters wrong.

you could say I was in the zone that day," Thompson later told Ross Atkin of the *Christian Science Monitor.*[36]

Thompson had seemingly locked up the scoring title: Gervin needed fifty-nine points to win it. The Iceman was not ready to concede the title, though. The Spurs had already won the division, so Gervin's teammates took it upon themselves to help him achieve his milestone.

The Iceman played only thirty-three minutes, but he made the most of his time on the court. He broke Thompson's newly established record for points in a quarter, scoring thirty-three in one period as he erupted for sixty-three points in the game. Gervin finished the season with an average of 27.21 points per game, edging out Thompson, who finished with 27.15. "It took all 12 guys to want me to do it in order for it to happen," Gervin told reporters after the game. "I was very nervous and missed my first six shots. But, my teammates . . . lit a fire under me. They were just as excited about it as I was. It's that relationship that made that moment so very special."[37]

A Legendary Career

Gervin may be best known for his epic scoring battle with Thompson, but there was much more to his career than that one season. Thompson later joked that Gervin "should have let me have that one [scoring crown] because he got three more after that."[38] The others came in 1978–1979 (29.6 points per game), 1979–1980 (33.1 ppg), and 1981–1982 (32.3 ppg). Gervin's offensive production places him in elite company. Only two other players, Wilt Chamberlain and Michael Jordan, have won at least four NBA scoring titles.

Indeed, the Iceman was a poker-faced scoring machine. *Sports Illustrated* writer Curry Kirkpatrick once observed, "As his moniker implies, Gervin does all this marvelous stuff while appearing to be in a deep coma—face expressionless, eyelids drooping, the Iceman to the letter."[39]

More than his visage, however, Gervin was known for his ability to put points on the board, especially late in the game when his team needed him most. "I consider the game won when Ice has his hands on the ball in that situation," former Spur Billy Paultz once said of his old teammate.[40]

Yet there was one thing the Iceman could never do—bring an NBA championship to San Antonio. Gervin was traded to the Chicago Bulls following the 1984–1985 season. When he parted ways with the Spurs, the thirty-three-year-old veteran held more than sixty team records. Gervin played in every game for the Bulls during the 1985–1986 season and averaged a respectable 16.2 points per game—second best on the team. Following the season, Chicago released him. He would not play in the NBA again.

Gervin retired from the National Basketball Association as a twelve-time ABA/NBA All-Star. He finished his NBA career with 20,708 points, a number that soars to 26,595 points when his ABA numbers are added. Gervin led San Antonio in scoring during eight of the nine NBA seasons he played with the team, and he was the Spurs' leading scorer in forty-seven of their seventy-five playoff games during that span. The Iceman also scored at least 1,000 points in thirteen consecutive seasons and retired as the Spurs' all-time leading scorer with 19,383 points and a career average of 26.3 points per game.

Life After the NBA

Even after the Bulls released him, basketball remained an important part of George Gervin's life. In 1986–1987 he played for Banco Roma, a team in the Italian League. Later, during the 1989–1990 season, he joined the Quad City Thunder of the Continental Basketball Association. But neither experience could match his days with the ABA and the NBA.

"Like many newly retired players, Gervin had trouble making the transition," states his biography at NBA.com. "He developed a cocaine habit that required three trips to rehabilitation clinics to break."[41]

In reality, Gervin had started using cocaine while still playing for the Spurs. But after he left the NBA his drug habit spiraled out of control. "I couldn't deal with not being in the league anymore," he admitted in a 1996 interview.[42] He ultimately turned to former teammate John Lucas for help, and he has since kicked the habit.

These days, Gervin splits his time between golf (he boasts a very respectable six handicap), family (he and his wife, Joyce,

Gervin (center) laughs with David Thompson (left) and Gail Goodrich just before their induction into the Basketball Hall of Fame in May 1996.

have three children), and charity work (his San Antonio–based youth center provides vocational training, mentoring, and a variety of other services for 1,400 families).

Basketball will always hold a special place in Gervin's heart. On December 5, 1987, the San Antonio Spurs retired the Iceman's number 44 jersey, and on February 3, 1995, he was inducted into the San Antonio Sports Hall of Fame. The following year, on May 6, 1996, the Iceman was enshrined in the Basketball Hall of Fame.

Gervin, who used the game he loved as a way to escape the ghettos of Detroit, has only fond memories of the sport. "Basketball is a great job, a fabulous job," he said. "Players should be thankful for getting paid big bucks to do something they truly love. How many people can say that about their jobs?"[43]

CHAPTER 4

Johnny Moore

Johnny Moore's career can be seen as both heroic and tragic. On the one hand, he overcame amazing odds to become an NBA star. On the other hand, his playing days were cut short by a rare illness. Moore was a determined and gutsy player who enjoyed a fine career with the Spurs.

The Kid from Altoona

Johnny Moore, the second son of Bill and June Moore, was born on March 31, 1958, in Altoona, Pennsylvania. Because he started kindergarten when he was only four years old, he was smaller than his classmates throughout elementary school.

When he was young, Johnny was interested in many sports, especially Little League baseball. However, he credits his older brother Billy, who was a basketball star at Altoona High School, with inspiring him to take up hoops. "Initially through the success he experienced," Johnny said, "I wanted to do the same thing he did. . . . I can remember how excited I was to see [Billy play] and how proud I was of my brother."[44]

Moore played basketball at Keith Junior High School and then followed in his brother's footsteps as a star for Altoona

Johnny Moore takes a shot during a University of Texas game. His accomplishments in college made NBA teams interested in the Texas guard.

High. At 5-foot-9 and 160 pounds, Moore was not built like a typical athlete. Thus, he was not heavily recruited during his senior year. That all changed, however, at the 1974 Dapper Dan Roundball Classic. His exceptional play impressed University of Texas coach Leon Black, who offered the seventeen-year-old Moore a scholarship. The kid from Altoona accepted and went to study and play in Austin, Texas.

Moore grew to 6-foot-1 and put on fifteen pounds during his first season with the Texas Longhorns, 1975–1976. After Moore's freshman year, however, Black was fired as coach and

Under Texas coach Abe Lemons, Moore grew into an outstanding point guard. He holds the Longhorns' career record for assists.

replaced by Abe Lemons. Lemons strongly believed in the importance of a talented point guard, and he saw the makings of a great one in Moore. "A lot of people don't appreciate a good guard," Lemons once said. "They don't understand he's the guy . . . who runs the team. You can't have a good team if you don't have a good guard."[45]

At first Moore, who was used to being a scorer, strongly resisted the idea that he was going to be the guy who helped everybody else score. Eventually, though, he came to like this role, and he excelled as a point guard for the Longhorns. During his four-year career at Texas, Moore started all 112 games and compiled 714 career assists, which remains a University of Texas record. He also dropped in 1,482 career points. Moore twice captured All-Southwest Conference (SWC) first-team honors, and twice he was named the Longhorns' MVP. In two different seasons he led the SWC in assists, and he still holds the conference's single-game assist record with nineteen—a feat he accomplished twice during the 1978–1979 season.

With Moore leading the way, the Longhorns won a pair of Southwest Conference co-championships and in 1978 were the National Invitational Tournament (NIT) champions. During Moore's senior season, Texas finished with a 21-8 record and made it to the second round of the NCAA tournament before falling to Oklahoma. His collegiate career had ended, but Moore had no regrets. "At that point," he said, "I felt like I accomplished what I went to Texas for, to establish it on the map as far as basketball was concerned."[46]

An Inauspicious Beginning

Moore had a tremendous impact on Longhorn basketball, but the reverse was also true. Thanks to Abe Lemons, Moore had grown to understand and appreciate the position he now played on a basketball court—that of point guard. "Sometimes it's hard because it looks like you're trying to make a star out of somebody else," claimed Lemons. "John was not receptive at first, but he learned a lot and it helped him down the line."[47]

Moore agreed. "Point guard isn't a position, it's a frame of mind," he said. "I see a lot of people who can handle the ball and bring it up the court, but they don't have a point guard frame of mind. You have to know tempo, who's hot, who's not. Once I realized I could destroy a team and not score, that helped me."[48]

However, nothing could have prepared Moore for the rocky start of his professional career. Though selected in the second round of the 1979 NBA draft by the Seattle SuperSonics, he never played a game for Seattle, which traded his draft rights to the San Antonio Spurs on June 26, 1979. Moore went through the Spurs' 1979 training camp and played well, but was cut by San Antonio coach Doug Moe. "He told me I did a good job, and did a lot of good things, but that he had to make a decision, and that Mike Evans was a little stronger," Moore recalled. "You've got to respect his opinion in that situation."[49]

Moore was out of basketball, but he refused to accept that his playing days were over. He returned to Austin and became an assistant coach with the Longhorns. He tried to stay in shape, but it was not always easy. "After a while, it got frustrating," Moore admitted. "I stopped working out. At that point, someone said if [an NBA team] called you today, you wouldn't be ready. I still wanted to give myself every opportunity, so I started working out again."[50]

As Moore sweated to stay in basketball shape, the Spurs were struggling through a dismal season. On March 1, 1980, Moe was fired as the team's coach. With just eight games left in the 1979–1980 season, interim San Antonio coach Bob Bass called Moore and offered him a second chance to play in the NBA. Needless to say, Moore accepted.

Rising from the Ashes

The 1980–1981 season was Moore's first full year with the Spurs. Coming off the bench as the backup to San Antonio great James Silas, Moore appeared in all eighty-two games and was on the floor for about nineteen minutes per game. He finished the regular season averaging 7.4 points, 4.5 assists, and 2.4 rebounds per game. Moore also shot nearly 48 percent from the field and 61 percent from the free-throw line. Despite his limited playing time, Moore averaged more assists per game than Silas, and he impressed new San Antonio coach Stan Albeck with his play during the postseason. Silas was traded after the season, and Moore was named the Spurs' new starting point guard.

Moore did not disappoint. He led the NBA in assists during the 1981–1982 season, dishing off 9.6 times per game. He also scored 9.4 points per game that season as San Antonio won the Midwest Division title. The Spurs repeated as division champions during the 1982–1983 season, and Moore was once again a driving force behind the club's success. That year, Moore averaged 12.2 points, 9.8 assists, and 3.6 rebounds per game. He also connected on 47 percent of his shots from the field and 74 percent of his free throws.

When San Antonio met the Denver Nuggets in the 1983 semifinals of the Western Conference, Moore welcomed the matchup: The Nuggets were coached by the man who had first cut him, Doug Moe. Moore let his offense do the talking, exploding for twenty-seven points and fourteen assists per game. In game three of the series, his thirty-nine-point outburst included the winning basket, a layup with twelve seconds remaining in overtime. "That was a really great feeling to have that type of impact," Moore recalled.[51]

San Antonio won the series and went on to play the Los Angeles Lakers in the Western Conference Finals. Moore again took control, dishing out ninety assists—an NBA playoff record—during the six-game

Moore emerged as San Antonio's starting point guard during the 1981–1982 season. He helped the Spurs win back-to-back Midwest Division titles.

series. However, the Lakers proved more than the Spurs could handle, knocking San Antonio out of the playoffs on the way to an NBA title.

San Antonio made a coaching change in the off-season, bringing in Morris McHone. But the 1983–1984 campaign would be a major disappointment for McHone, the Spurs, and Johnny Moore. San Antonio limped out of the gate, and, as his team continued to struggle, McHone was replaced by Spurs general manager Bob Bass. San Antonio finished the season

Moore's best season was 1984–1985, when he averaged 12.8 points, 10 assists, and 2.8 steals per game and helped San Antonio earn a playoff berth.

with a 37-45 record, failing to make the playoffs for the first time since Moore had joined the team. That was not the point guard's only disappointment, however. Moore, playing in just fifty-nine games, saw his scoring, rebounding, and assist averages all drop.

Cotton Fitzsimmons took over as the Spurs' coach the following season, and the team's fortunes improved somewhat. Though San Antonio managed just a 41-41 record in 1984–1985, the Spurs returned to the playoffs. Moore also enjoyed a personally satisfying season. For the first time in his NBA career, he started all eighty-two games, racking up a career-high 2,689 minutes and 1,046 points (12.8 per game). Moore also managed career bests with 378 rebounds (4.6 per game), 816 assists (10.0 per game), and 229 steals (2.8 per game). Moore and the Spurs again met Moe and the Nuggets in the playoffs in the spring of 1985, but this time Denver got the better of San Antonio, eliminating the Spurs in five games. Regardless, Moore and the rest of the team seemed to be headed in the right direction again.

Illness Strikes

On December 21, 1985, Moore woke up at 5 A.M. so he could prepare for San Antonio's upcoming regular-season game against the Nuggets. It was at this time that he first noticed that something was physically wrong with him. "When I woke up," he recalled, "it was as if I had [drunk] a gallon of booze or something. . . . I could just tell it wasn't a regular headache, but I went to Denver and played anyway."[52]

Despite feeling under the weather, Moore played exceptionally well. He scored 22 points and added 11 assists in a 128-118 victory. "That night in Denver was the highlight of Johnny's career," said Bass.[53] But every time Moore exited the game for a breather, he appeared to be in agony on the bench.

Five days later, during a team shoot-around, Coach Fitzsimmons looked over and saw Moore on the bench, in obvious pain from another headache. "I knew then, when he was hurting too much to shoot around, that those weren't just ordinary headaches," Fitzsimmons told *Denver Post* reporter Jim Armstrong. "I stopped things right there and said, 'Let's get to the bottom of this.'"[54] Moore was taken to Humana Hospital in San

Antonio, where tests were run to find the cause of his intense headaches.

The news was not good: Moore had coccidioidomycosis, or "desert fever," a rare form of meningitis. The symptoms of this serious illness include fever, chest pain, chills, the coughing up of blood, and inflammation of the eyes and joints. An infection around the brain was what was causing Moore's headaches. Certain forms of desert fever can be fatal, but doctors assured Moore that he could beat the disease. It would be an uphill battle, though. "What Moore has on his hands is a recovery period that, according to his physician, Dr. Richard Thorner, could last as long as two years," wrote Armstrong.[55]

The treatments Moore underwent were excruciating. On January 15, 1986, doctors drilled a hole in his skull. Through the hole they inserted a device that released medicine to help relieve Moore's pain. He was placed on another medication that fought the infection but also made him severely nauseated. After more than a month in the hospital, Moore was finally released, and instantly his thoughts turned toward a return to basketball. To those who knew him, and knew what he had already been through during his NBA career, this did not come as a surprise. "Johnny will be all right, we just know it," said teammate Mike Mitchell. "Johnny's spirits always stay up."[56]

Added Bass, "He went through a lot just to stick in this league. Let me tell you something about Johnny Moore: He's a survivor."[57]

A Heroic Return

Amazingly, Johnny Moore was able to return to basketball for the 1986–1987 season. Moore played fifty-five games that season but averaged just twenty-two minutes per game. He scored 474 points (an average of 8.6 points per game) while adding 250 assists (4.5 per game) and 100 rebounds (1.8 per game). Clearly, his play was not at the level it had been before the illness. Still, the fact that he was back on the court a full year ahead of his doctor's expectations was amazing.

The following season, 1987–1988, the Spurs released Moore after five games. Again, though, he refused to give up. He played one game with the New Jersey Nets that season and continued to work out and practice. He also continued to battle the symptoms of desert fever.

Moore had one last comeback in him. He signed with the Spurs again on November 22, 1989, and played in fifty-three games for San Antonio during the 1989–1990 season, averaging 2.2 points and 1.5 assists per game. On August 23, 1990, he was again released by the Spurs. This time, there would be no more comebacks. Johnny Moore's basketball career was over.

Johnny Moore guards Michael Jordan early in the 1986–1987 season. Moore's return to basketball after contracting desert fever amazed doctors.

A Career Worth Remembering

Moore has worn many hats since leaving the NBA as a player. In 1993, he joined the Spurs' Community Relations Department, and he has spoken at hundreds of schools, churches, and charitable events. "It keeps me busy," Moore said. "I get a chance to go out, see the kids and try to make a positive contribution."[58] He received a degree in sociology in May of 1997. He is married and has a daughter.

As for basketball, Moore has turned his ambitions in another direction. "Coaching is something I'd like to get into," he said. "I think I can be very effective. The Spurs obviously are my first choice, but, down the road, I might have to leave town and start that career elsewhere."[59]

Moore enjoyed a solid playing career. He retired as the Spurs' all-time assist leader with 3,685 and was second in team history with 1,017 steals. He also holds the franchise single-game playoff record for assists with twenty, a mark he set against the Nuggets in 1983. On March 20, 1988, his number 00 became just the third number ever retired by the Spurs, and in 2003, he was inducted into the San Antonio Sports Hall of Fame.

Still, one cannot help but wonder what Moore's career would have been like had he never been stricken with desert fever. Moore himself sometimes thinks about that. "I feel blessed . . . to have been able to play the game I love," he said. "But I feel that I didn't have time to accomplish what I feel I could have accomplished. That's a little unsettling to me. . . . But I focus on the good things I have. You have a lot of twists and turns in your life and you have to adapt to them."[60]

Johnny Moore faced the twists and turns of his life with a unique courage and determination that makes his career worth remembering.

CHAPTER 5

David Robinson

David Robinson was the first graduate of the United States Naval Academy ever to play professional basketball. He spent fourteen seasons in the NBA—all of them with San Antonio. When he retired after the 2002–2003 season, Robinson could claim numerous team records, including career marks for most games played, most points, most rebounds, and most blocked shots. Despite his great basketball achievements, the game was rarely the most important thing to this down-to-earth man, who was a dedicated student throughout his youth and even opted to temporarily put his athletic ambitions on hold in order to serve his country in the military.

An Unlikely Start

On August 6, 1965, in Key West, Florida, Freda Robinson gave birth to a baby boy, David Maurice. David was the second child of Freda and her husband, Ambrose, and the couple's first boy. Ambrose worked as a senior chief sonar technician in the U.S. Navy, and his job soon took the family to Norfolk, Virginia, the site of an important naval base. That is where David spent most of his childhood.

David Robinson slams a shot home. Robinson spent fourteen seasons in the NBA, and in 1996 he was voted one of the fifty greatest NBA players of all time.

David Robinson proved early on that he was a very bright child. By the third grade, he had already been placed in gifted classes, and in junior high he began taking college courses in mathematics and computer science. He seemed to have a natural ability for academics.

The same could not be said for basketball, however. David first decided to try the sport while in junior high. The 5-foot-9 youth played sparingly, and, fearing that the sport would interfere with his studies, he opted to give it up. He would not play organized basketball again until his family moved to Manassas, Virginia, a suburb of Washington, D.C., before his senior year of high school. By this time, Robinson, now a student at Osbourn Park High School in Manassas, had grown to 6-foot-7. He did not have a passion for the game at this point in his life, but Osbourn Park basketball coach Art Payne convinced him to try out for the team. Robinson joined the squad as a backup center, but an injury to a teammate soon placed him in the starting lineup. He made the most of the opportunity and played well that season.

Robinson began getting some attention from college scouts, many of whom were impressed by his raw talent but saw him as a project because he was new to the game. Robinson already had plans for his post-secondary education, though. He wanted to attend the United States Naval Academy in Annapolis, Maryland, and then enter the service like his father. Even though Robinson—who had scored 1320 out of a possible 1600 on his SAT exams—had his heart set on Navy, his father encouraged him to consider other options. Naval Academy graduates were required to serve five years in the military, and Ambrose Robinson worried that the service commitment would ruin David's chance to play professional basketball. David, who at the time had no interest in an NBA career, recalls that his father was "the only one who saw the player I could become. . . . He said to me, 'You sure you want that five-year commitment?' But . . . I couldn't see myself as a pro basketball player. So I went."[61]

Cadet Robinson Reports for Duty

Robinson maintained a grueling schedule during his freshman year at the Academy. He had classes in advanced calculus, naval history, weapons systems, and other subjects. Each class brought with it mountains of homework. On top of his studies, there was an Academy-mandated physical fitness regimen, as well as basketball practice. Somehow, Robinson managed to juggle his intense workload.

On the court, the Academy's team was very successful. The 1983–1984 Navy basketball team topped the twenty-win mark for the first time in the school's history. Robinson played in twenty-eight games that season, averaging fewer than eight points per game and managing just four rebounds for the entire season. He still lacked a love for the game, calling basketball "more work than fun."[62]

During Robinson's sophomore year, 1984–1985, he began to break out as a player. He shattered a United States Naval

Academy record by scoring 756 points, leading Navy to a 26-6 record and its first berth in the NCAA tournament in twenty-five years. The highlight of Robinson's second year at the Academy, however, came during the week of the Saluki Shootout tournament. During that tournament he became the first Navy player in eighteen years to score more than thirty points in consecutive games, a feat that won him the tournament's Most Valuable Player award. Robinson called the experience "pretty incredible. . . . It was the first time I got an idea of what I could do."[63]

By his senior year, Robinson was the most dominant center in college basketball, averaging 28.2 points, 11.8 rebounds, and 4.5 blocked shots per game for Navy.

At this point in his career, Robinson considered transferring. If he left the Naval Academy before the start of his junior year, he would be able to escape his five-year service commitment. Several schools, including basketball powers UCLA, Kentucky, Georgetown, and Indiana, expressed interest in Robinson. In response, Navy brass hinted that, if Robinson chose to stay, he might be rewarded with a reduced military obligation. Robinson did decide to stay. As he told his coach, Paul Evans, "I like basketball, and it's a challenge, but it is one of a number of parts of my life. If I have to, I can live without it."[64]

Robinson made the most of his remaining days at Navy. During the 1985–1986 season, Navy went 30-5 and won its second straight Colonial Conference championship. Robinson averaged nearly twenty-three points and thirteen rebounds per game and set NCAA records for most shots blocked in a game (14), a season (207), and a career (372). By his senior year, Robinson had grown to 7-foot-1. That season, he led the league in blocked shots, averaging 4.5 blocks per game, and was third in the NCAA in scoring average (28.2 points per game) and fourth in rebounding (11.8 per game). Robinson won the Naismith Award as the best college player of the year after the 1986–1987 season, and he finished his career with thirty-three Naval Academy records, including most career points (2,669) and most career rebounds (1,314).

The news was not all good for him, however. During the season, Secretary of the Navy John F. Lehman had ruled that Robinson, because he was too tall to serve on a naval vessel, would only have to serve for two years after graduation, and he would be permitted to play in the NBA should he be stationed near the team that drafted him. However, following the end of Robinson's senior year, Lehman resigned and was replaced by James H. Webb. Webb overturned Lehman's ruling, decreeing that athletes like Robinson would not be given special treatment. Robinson's height would still mean that he had to serve just two years of active duty, but he would not be allowed to play professional basketball during that time. The NBA would have to wait.

Robinson, to his credit, took the news in stride. He insisted that he did not regret his decision to attend Annapolis, saying instead, "Things turned out for me real well. . . . I can't complain at all."[65]

Robinson graduated from the Naval Academy in May 1987. On June 22, the San Antonio Spurs made him the first pick in the NBA draft. Just weeks later, Ensign Robinson reported to the King's Bay Naval Submarine Base in Georgia, where he worked for the next two years as a civil engineer overseeing construction projects.

Robinson had few chances to play basketball while fulfilling his commitment to the navy, and his game suffered. He was a member of the U.S. teams that participated in the 1987 Pan American Games and the 1988 Olympics, but on both occasions he played poorly. Robinson was discharged from the military on May 19, 1989, and he immediately turned his attention to the NBA.

The Admiral Arrives

The Spurs team that Robinson joined in 1989 was quite different from the one that had drafted him in 1987. During those two years, owner Angelo Drossos had sold the team to Red McCombs. The team, which had gone 21-61 during the 1988–1989 season, had also made a coaching change. New head coach Larry Brown pulled the trigger on several key trades, including the acquisitions of Terry Cummings and Maurice Cheeks, to help strengthen the club. Robinson worked hard during the off-season, attending various camps in order to get himself back into basketball shape. When it came time to start the 1989 season, both Robinson and the Spurs were ready to give their best.

In Robinson's first NBA game, against the Los Angeles Lakers, he scored twenty-three points and pulled down seventeen rebounds in a 106-98 San Antonio victory. Robinson's play was so impressive that after the game Lakers great Magic Johnson told reporters, "Some rookies are never really rookies. Robinson's one of them."[66]

In the 1989–1990 season, Robinson started eighty-one of the team's eighty-two games. He connected on better than 53 percent of his shots, averaging 24.3 points per game; he also pulled down 12 rebounds per game and recorded 3.89 blocks per game. Thanks to his contributions, the Spurs won the Midwest Division crown with a 56-26 record. The team won thirty-five more games than in the previous year—the best single-season turnaround in league history—and Robinson took home NBA Rookie of the Year honors for leading the way.

Brown was amazed not just by Robinson's talent, but by his leadership as well. "What's happened is that, in one season, this has become David's team," the coach said. "He is its heart and soul. . . . the more he grows into that role, the better he'll become and the better the team will become."[67]

That first season was indeed a sign of great things to come from the man nicknamed "the Admiral" (a reference to his navy background). During the 1990–1991 year, he improved in every conceivable category, upping his scoring average to 25.6 points per game while connecting on 55 percent of his shots and averaging 13 rebounds and 3.9 blocks per game. Robinson won the NBA rebounding title that season and was named an All-Star and a member of the All-Defensive First Team. With Robinson leading the way, the Spurs won fifty-five games and claimed the Midwest Division for the second straight year. Basketball experts felt that Robinson and the Spurs had a good chance to win their first NBA championship, but San Antonio was upset by Golden State in the first round of the playoffs. For Robinson, playoff disappointment would be repeated many times during his career.

A Complete Performer

As the 1991–1992 season opened, expectations were high for Robinson and the Spurs. Initially, San Antonio delivered. The club began the season by winning ten of its first thirteen games. The team struggled in December and January, however, leading Brown to resign as coach.

The Spurs recovered under new coach Bob Bass and rallied to finish second in the division with a 47-35 record. Once again, Robinson enjoyed a great season, especially on defense. He was named the NBA's Defensive Player of the Year and became San Antonio's all-time career leader in blocked shots. Robinson's season came to a premature end, however, when he tore a ligament in his left hand in March. Without their big man, the

Robinson splits Phoenix defenders Charles Barkley (left) and John Williams to take a shot.

Spurs were swept by the Phoenix Suns in the first round of the playoffs.

Robinson had proven his defensive prowess during the 1991–1992 season. During the 1993–1994 season, he showed what an offensive threat he could be. The off-season acquisition of Dennis Rodman, a rebounding specialist, allowed Robinson to focus more on his scoring. He averaged 29.8 points per game and, in the final contest of the season, scored a career-high seventy-one points against the Los Angeles Clippers. Robinson won the NBA scoring title that season and became just the fourth player in league history to record a quadruple-double (double figures in points, rebounds, assists, and blocked shots), doing so in a game against the Detroit Pistons. Robinson had proven he could be a complete player, dominant both on offense and defense.

The following season, 1994–1995, would be Robinson's finest as a professional. On November 7, 1994, he scored his ten-thousandth career point in a 105-96 win over the New Jersey Nets. On January 1, 1995, he became the first player in franchise history to collect five thousand career rebounds. For the season Robinson averaged 27.6 points, 10.8 rebounds, 2.9 assists, and 3.23 blocks per game. Those numbers, combined with his leadership on the floor, earned him the NBA's Most Valuable Player honors.

Although Robinson powered San Antonio to the league's best regular-season record (62-20), in the playoffs the Spurs again came up short. San Antonio fell to the eventual NBA champion Houston Rockets in the Western Conference Finals.

David Robinson had clearly established himself as a star by averaging more than twenty points, ten rebounds, and three blocks per game in each of his first seven seasons. In 1996, as the NBA celebrated its fiftieth anniversary, Robinson was named one of the league's fifty greatest players of all time. However, he had yet to lead San Antonio to an NBA title. Worse yet, injuries limited him to six games during the 1996–1997 season. He missed the first eighteen games with a back strain and then missed the final fifty-eight games of the campaign with a fracture in his left foot. Without their best player the Spurs struggled to a 20-62 record and missed the playoffs. Robinson's chances of ever winning a championship seemed slim.

Help was on the way, though. After the dreadful 1996–1997 season, the Spurs chose Tim Duncan with the top pick in the draft.

Good Things Come to Those Who Wait

Duncan made an immediate impact in 1997–1998, teaming with Robinson to lead San Antonio to a 56-26 record. Robinson played seventy-three games that season, averaging 21.6 points and 10.6 rebounds per game. He finished tenth in the league in scoring, fifth in rebounding, and fifth in shot blocking while also ranking among the NBA's most accurate shooters by connecting on 51 percent of his field-goal attempts. Duncan, meanwhile, won the NBA's Rookie of the Year award by hitting almost 55 percent of his shots, averaging 21.1 points per game, and pulling down a season total of 977 rebounds.

With the "Twin Towers" (as the duo had been dubbed) leading the way, San Antonio finished second in the Midwest Division. According to coach Gregg Popovich, the key to the tandem's success was the freedom they had on the court. "The last thing we wanted to do was preordain where they would be on the floor and try to fit them into some preconceived notion of what should happen," Popovich said. "We wanted to see how they react to each other."[68] The results were impressive, and they were only going to get better.

The 1998–1999 season started late because of a contract dispute between NBA players and team owners. When the lockout ended, the Spurs stumbled to a 6-8 start. However, Robinson sensed that Duncan was maturing as a player, and he unselfishly stepped aside to allow the second-year star to shine. That season, Duncan led San Antonio with 21.7 points, 11.4 rebounds, and 2.52 blocked shots per game. With Duncan, not Robinson, leading the way, San Antonio won thirty-one of its last thirty-six games to become Midwest Division champions. The team's dominance continued in the postseason, as the Spurs won eleven out of their first twelve playoff games to reach the NBA Finals, where they upended the New York Knicks in five games.

The "Twin Towers," David Robinson and Tim Duncan, defend New York's
Latrell Sprewell during the fifth game of the 1999 NBA Finals.

Robinson remained more of a defensive weapon than an offensive threat during the Finals. In the last game against the
Knicks, he scored fifteen points and pulled down twelve rebounds. Many saw Robinson's willingness to let Duncan star
as the biggest contribution to the team's success that season.
"Robinson swallowed his pride, stepped aside, and let the
emerging Duncan become the team's featured scoring threat,
while himself assuming the role of defensive leader," wrote
Craig Daniels of the *Toronto Sun* after the Spurs won the NBA

David Robinson walks with his sons Corey and Justin following a news conference during which he announced his retirement.

title. "In so doing, he set in motion the events that led to a league-best 37-13 record and, ultimately, last night's victory."[69]

After a long and successful career, David Robinson had finally become an NBA champion. He described the feeling as overwhelming. "One minute you're still climbing that mountain, and the next minute everything you've been working for is right there in your possession. The suddenness of it can throw you for a loop," he wrote after the Finals victory. "I've been at this for so long—10 years in the NBA—that all my emotion just wasn't going to come out in one moment. I still have to get used to the idea that there's nobody left to beat. It's going to take me a month to exhale."[70] Unbeknownst to Spurs fans, shortly after the team won the NBA title Robinson began to consider retirement.

A Life Beyond Basketball

Robinson played in all eighty-two of his team's games during the 1999–2000 season, averaging 17.8 points and 9.60 rebounds per game in around thirty-two minutes per night. His playing time, scoring, and rebounding averages decreased steadily during each of the next three seasons, but this did little to tarnish his legacy as one of the best players ever to step onto an NBA court. Injuries and age were beginning to catch up to him, and before the 2002–2003 season, he decided that his fourteenth NBA season would be his last. He would go out in style, helping to lead the Spurs to their second NBA championship.

Robinson retired as the Spurs' career leader in scoring, rebounding, blocked shots, and assists. But he will be remembered for much more than just his basketball prowess. On December 23, 1992, Robinson and his wife, Valerie, created the David Robinson Foundation, an organization supporting programs that aid families and children. In September of 1997, Robinson used a $5 million endowment to establish the Carver Academy, an independent school for disadvantaged children. In 1998, he was inducted into the World Sports Humanitarian Hall of Fame.

On the eve of his retirement from the game, the NBA announced that it would name the league's Community Service Award in honor of the Admiral. "He is truly a class guy and a great representative for his team and the league," said Houston Rockets coach Rudy Tomjanovich. "I admire him greatly."[71]

Orlando Magic coach Doc Rivers agreed. "I don't think anyone," Rivers said, "will ever mean more to San Antonio than David Robinson."[72]

CHAPTER 6

Tim Duncan

Tim Duncan suffered through many hardships as a young-ster, but his determination led him to an outstanding career at Wake Forest University and to NBA stardom. A former NBA Rookie of the Year and two-time Most Valuable Player, Duncan has guided the San Antonio Spurs to many on-court successes. However, it is not just his play, but also his many charitable works around the San Antonio area, that have won him a place in the hearts of many people.

A Difficult Childhood

Tim Duncan was born in St. Croix, the Virgin Islands, on April 25, 1976. His sisters, Cheryl and Tricia, were both talented swimmers who greatly inspired their younger brother. When Tricia Duncan was fourteen years old, she qualified for the 1988 Summer Olympics in the backstroke. Tim admired his older sis-ters, so it was only natural that he also loved to swim. At the age of ten, he decided to start training for the Olympics as well. By the time he was thirteen, Tim had become a top swimmer in the 400-meter freestyle. His sister Tricia claims that the future basketball star was actually the best swimmer in the family.

"Timmy was even better than me," she once told *Sports Illustrated* writer Tim Crothers. "There is no doubt in my mind that he would have gone to the 1992 Olympics and held his own against the world."[73]

Duncan never got the chance to find out if he could have competed against Olympic-caliber swimmers. On the evening of September 18, 1989, Hurricane Hugo pounded St. Croix, leveling buildings, ripping down power lines, and transforming the island into a disaster area. The storm left the Duncans' hometown of Christiansted in ruins. In addition to the many homes and buildings it had wrecked, the hurricane destroyed the pool Tim Duncan had used for training. Because it was the only swimming complex on the entire island and because the ocean water was deemed too full of bacteria to be safe for swimming, Duncan had to put his training on hold.

Tim Duncan, who won the NBA's Most Valuable Player award after the 2001–2002 and 2002–2003 seasons, is arguably the league's best player.

Shortly after the hurricane, the Duncan clan suffered an even more devastating blow when Ione Duncan, Tim's mother, was diagnosed with breast cancer. Ione's illness consumed Tim's thoughts. She was being treated in Red Cross tents because of hurricane damage to the hospital. Ione fought cancer valiantly but died in April 1990, one day before Tim's fourteenth birthday. Duncan would never swim competitively again. "The hurricane broke Tim's routine by taking away our pool," Tricia later said. "Then when mom passed, he lost his motivation [to swim]."[74]

Discovering Basketball

Duncan might have never become interested in basketball if not for his sister Cheryl. For Christmas in 1988, Cheryl gave Tim a pole, backboard, and hoop. She and her husband, Rick Lowery, a former guard for Division III Capital University in Ohio, also encouraged Tim. Lowery first met his wife's brother when Tim was a 6-foot-1 ninth grader. Impressed with the youth's skills, Lowery worked with him, playing one-on-one and two-on-two games. Young Tim Duncan also learned from other players on the island. Lowery eventually convinced Tim to join the basketball team at St. Dunstan's Episcopal High School.

While in high school, Duncan caught the eye of former Wake Forest star Chris King, who was playing with a group of NBA draft choices touring St. Croix as part of a goodwill tour. King did not catch Duncan's name, but he was impressed by how well the youth played against former Georgetown center Alonzo Mourning. King told Wake Forest coach Dave Odom, and an excited Odom sent an assistant coach to the island on a fact-finding mission. Within days, Odom knew all about Duncan and traveled to St. Croix to see the youngster play. "As I watched him for the first time," Odom recalls, "I was impressed by his poise and composure and his presence on the court. He was . . . not an overly imposing player, but you could tell he had earned the respect of the older players out there."[75]

Thanks to Odom's persistence—and some helpful advice from Lowery—Duncan eventually decided to attend Wake Forest. The seventeen-year-old entered the university as a young player in need of a lot of coaching. He went scoreless in his first college game (a loss to Division II Alaska-Anchorage), but his play rapidly improved. During his freshman season, Duncan averaged 9.8 points and 9.6 rebounds per game, and he set a school record with 124 blocked shots.

During his sophomore year with the Demon Deacons, he averaged nearly seventeen points per game and led Wake Forest to its first Atlantic Coast Conference (ACC) title in thirty-three years. His junior season brought Duncan a lot of national attention, as he averaged 19.1 points per game and helped the Demon

Deacons repeat as ACC champions. He led Wake Forest to three NCAA tournament victories, but the team fell to the Kentucky Wildcats in the round of eight.

Despite pressure to leave college early and enter the NBA draft, Duncan returned to school for his senior season. He averaged 20.8 points per game during the 1996–1997 campaign. Wake Forest won thirteen in a row to start the season before

Duncan slams the ball home during a 1996 NCAA tournament game. While at Wake Forest University, Duncan emerged as one of the best college players.

finally losing a game. Duncan once again led his team into the NCAA tournament, but his college career ended with a disappointing loss to Stanford in the second round. "We wanted to go further in the tournament, not just for the team but for Tim," recalled former Wake Forest player Jerry Braswell. "He's done a lot for this program and a lot for this team, and we wanted him to go out with something good on his back."[76]

Duncan's days at Wake Forest may have ended on a sour note, but he had compiled impressive career statistics. He was the first player in NCAA history to finish with more than 1,500 points, 1,000 rebounds, 400 blocks, and 200 assists. He also was a two-time ACC Player of the Year, a two-time Associated Press first-team All-American, a three-time National Defensive Player of the Year, and the consensus NCAA Player of the Year for the 1996–1997 season. Now it was time for the kid from St. Croix to try his luck in the NBA.

The Twin Towers Are Born

The San Antonio Spurs won the draft lottery in 1997 and made no secret that Tim Duncan would be the first overall selection. The forward/center from Wake Forest would step in immediately and team with San Antonio center David Robinson to form an intimidating frontcourt presence. Duncan quickly proved his worth to the franchise, scoring nineteen points and collecting twenty-two boards in an early-season game against the powerhouse Chicago Bulls. Although the Spurs lost the game, Duncan and Robinson stifled the low-post game of the legendary Michael Jordan. "I tried to get to the basket," Jordan observed after the game. "But with those two twin towers sitting in the middle, it was tough."[77]

Duncan was selected to play in the NBA All-Star Game and won Rookie of the Month honors for every month during the entire season. It came as no surprise when he also won the NBA's Rookie of the Year award. Over the course of the 1997–1998 season he had averaged 21.1 points per game, shot nearly 55 percent from the floor, and garnered 977 rebounds, 224 assists, and 206 blocks. Duncan also made the NBA's All-Defensive Second Team, becoming just the fifth rookie in league history to do so.

The combination of Duncan's size and his athletic ability make him a powerful force on both offense and defense. Here he blocks a shot by New Jersey's Richard Jefferson.

"I have seen the future and he wears 21," NBA great Charles Barkley said after facing Duncan during the season. "He's even better than I thought he was, and I was expecting good stuff."[78]

The individual accolades were nothing new, and as nice as it was to receive recognition for his basketball talents, the one thing Duncan had never won, at any level, was a team championship. His "Twin Tower" teammate, David Robinson, had played ten seasons in the NBA and had yet to win a title. Duncan did not intend to wait that long.

Taking Charge

Entering the 1998–1999 season Duncan and Robinson had a full year of playing together under their belts, and the two had learned how to work together effectively on the basketball court. The Admiral was most impressed by Duncan's ability to learn. "Tim has an incredibly quick mind," Robinson observed. "You show him something once and you'll never have to show him again."[79]

The duo would have to wait to show off their improved chemistry, as a player lockout and contract dispute delayed the start of the NBA season. Once play did get under way, Duncan and the Spurs dominated, going 37-13 in the shortened season and tying the Utah Jazz for the league's best record. Duncan led San Antonio with 21.7 points, 11.4 rebounds, and 2.52 blocked shots per game, and he was named to the All-NBA First Team and the NBA All-Defensive First Team. He was seventh in the league in scoring, fifth in rebounding, and seventh in shot blocking. Duncan also connected on 49.5 percent of his field-goal attempts, good for eighth in the league.

Duncan shone brightest in the playoffs, however. The Spurs easily defeated Minnesota, Los Angeles, and Portland to reach the NBA Finals. There, they battled the Eastern Conference champion New York Knicks. The Knicks played well, but they were no match for the Spurs. Duncan averaged twenty-four points and seventeen rebounds per game in the Finals, scoring more than thirty points twice during the five-game series as San Antonio won the title. For his heroics, the second-year star was named Most Valuable Player of the series.

"I don't think there are words to describe Tim Duncan," Spurs forward Sean Elliott told the Associated Press after the final game. "He's not flashy, he's not in your face, he doesn't have to intimidate people. He just goes out and plays the game with a lot of style, a lot of class."[80]

Duncan viewed winning the Finals MVP award as "an incredible honor. But all it means is that they're going to come at you harder next time. All you do is get a high off it all summer and come back at it next year."[81] No one doubted that Duncan would come back at it next year, and many of his rivals worried that the best might still be forthcoming from this phenom.

Maturing into Stardom

The Spurs had another good season in 1999–2000, finishing with a 53-29 record. Duncan continued to excel. For the second consecutive season, he was named to the All-NBA First Team and the All-Defensive First Team. He played in seventy-four games and averaged 23.2 points, 12.4 rebounds, 3.2 assists, and 2.23 blocks per game. He shot 49 percent from the field and a career-high 76 percent from the foul line. However, the Spurs failed to repeat as NBA champions, suffering elimination in the first round of the playoffs.

Duncan, who has been dubbed "the Big Fundamental" by Shaquille O'Neal, drew a lot of comparisons with the Lakers center during the 1999–2000 season—not so much in their styles of play, but in the results each produced. Duncan and O'Neal were the only two players that season to rank among the NBA's top ten in scoring, rebounds, and blocks. Duncan

Duncan (number 21) and his Spurs teammates celebrate after defeating the New York Knicks, 78–77, to win the NBA championship on June 25, 1999.

Tim Duncan grabs a rebound in front of Los Angeles Lakers star Shaquille O'Neal. The two big men can each dominate a game, although in different ways.

dropped in twenty-four points and snagged twenty-four rebounds in the All-Star Game and was named co-MVP of the contest, sharing the honor with O'Neal. Duncan was second in the NBA—behind only Shaq—with sixty double-doubles. During the season, Duncan also posted his first career triple-double, scoring seventeen points and adding seventeen rebounds and eleven assists against the Cleveland Cavaliers on March 25, 2000.

Duncan started all eighty-two of San Antonio's games the following season, posting 22.2 points, 12.2 rebounds, 3.0 assists, and 2.34 blocked shots per game. During the 2000–2001 season, he was fourteenth in the NBA in scoring, fourth in rebounding, seventh in shot blocking, and twelfth in field goal percentage. He led the league with sixty-six double-doubles, and he even had five 20-20 games during the season, including twenty-three points and a regular-season best twenty-three rebounds against the Sacramento Kings on December 5. (He would snag twenty-three rebounds again later in the season against Portland.) In addition, Duncan scored more than thirty points in ten different games, including a season-high forty-two against the Kings on April 12. When Duncan started his third straight All-Star Game, he scored fourteen points in twenty-eight minutes.

Tim Duncan had matured into an exceptional basketball player, all the while maintaining a quiet, professional demeanor. As Barkley said, "You don't have to talk trash when you are as good as he is."[82] Four times in his career, Duncan had finished in the top five in voting for the Maurice Podoloff Trophy, awarded each year to the NBA's Most Valuable Player. Now, the Big Fundamental was about to take his game to an entirely new level.

Simply the Best

San Antonio finished with a 58-24 record in 2001–2002, the same record the team had compiled in the previous season. The Spurs also won their second straight Midwest Division crown. Once again, it was Duncan who led the way. He averaged 25.5 points, 12.7 rebounds, 3.7 assists, and 2.48 blocks while playing every game. He scored thirty or more points twenty times, including a career-high fifty-three points against the Dallas Mavericks on December 26. He ranked in the NBA's top ten in five major statistical categories, including rebounding (second), blocked shots (third), and scoring (fifth), becoming just the fifth player since the 1972–1973 season to rank in the top five in those three categories. Duncan also led the NBA in field goals made, free throws made, and double-doubles. He was selected to the All-NBA First Team for the fifth straight time, becoming just the sixth player in league history to receive that honor in each of his first five years.

Duncan was one of the favorites to win the 2002 MVP award, but he had been overlooked before, particularly after San Antonio's championship season. Duncan's teammates had been angry when he was not selected as the league's Most Valuable Player after the magical 1998–1999 title run. "He's obviously the MVP of the league this year," Elliott had told reporters after the 1998–1999 Finals. "You guys who didn't vote for him should be ashamed of yourself."[83]

David Robinson (right) holds up the NBA Championship trophy while Duncan lifts the Finals MVP trophy after San Antonio defeated the New Jersey Nets to win the 2003 title.

Duncan would not be overlooked in 2002. In one of the closest votes ever, he captured the Podoloff Trophy. He received 57 first-place votes and 954 points to edge out Jason Kidd of the Nets, who received 45 first-place votes and 897 points.

Most observers agreed that Duncan was the NBA's best player. "You can't really guard him," said Houston coach Rudy Tomjanovich. "He has no weaknesses you can exploit."[84]

Writer David DuPree of *USA Today*, calling Duncan "as complete a player as the NBA has," shared this assessment. "He knows how to get position in the post and hold it and he has the most varied inside game of any NBA big man," DuPree wrote. "His release on his shot is quick, and he gets so close to defenders it's difficult for them to block any of his shots. He also runs the floor extremely well."[85]

The Total Package

Tim Duncan knows there is more to life than basketball. He is very active in charitable causes. In December of 2001, he and his wife, Amy, decided to create an organization that would help him give back to the community of San Antonio. The Tim Duncan Foundation, as it was dubbed, has supplied funds to a variety of nonprofit organizations, including those in the education, health awareness, and youth sports areas.

Throughout his Spurs career, Duncan has spearheaded a variety of charity events. His annual Charity Bowl-A-Thon has raised more than $350,000 to fight breast and prostate cancer. Through the SlamDuncan Charity Golf Classic, the Tim Duncan Foundation has donated more than $50,000 to Kids Sports Network, a nonprofit group that promotes quality sports opportunities for children. In 2001, the NBA recognized Duncan for his commitment to the community by honoring him with the Home Team Community Service Award. The award, which included a $25,000 donation to the cause of Tim's choice, the San Antonio Children's Shelter, came as no surprise to those who know Duncan. "He's just rock solid and dependable in every aspect of his life," remarked his agent, Lon Babby, "and it's been gratifying watching his evolution as a decision maker both on and off the court."[86]

The 2002–2003 season was typical of Duncan's life and career in the NBA. He once again put up astounding numbers on the court, averaging career bests in rebounds, assists, and blocked shots and winning his second MVP award. He was also named Most Valuable Player of the NBA Finals, as the Spurs won their second championship. Off the court, Duncan teamed with the Spurs and SBC (a telecommunications company affiliated with the basketball team) for the Tim Duncan ArtBall project, which sold basketballs painted by local artists. Proceeds went to the nonprofit Brighton School of San Antonio, which provides services for children with disabilities.

As a child, Tim Duncan saw a hurricane level his home and suffered through the loss of his mother. Despite these hardships, he has become the best player in professional basketball and one of the NBA's most dedicated community leaders.

CHAPTER 7

Tony Parker

A t first glance, Tony Parker may seem like an odd candidate for basketball stardom. Yet the young point guard, who learned the game in his native France, stands out as one of the best European players in the NBA today.

After a short but stellar career in France, Parker quickly showed off his raw talent as a member of the San Antonio Spurs. Parker has won the respect and admiration of his teammates, and he may be a key member of the San Antonio backcourt for years to come.

Basketball in His Blood

Tony Parker did not always have basketball in his heart, but he did have it in his blood. Born William Anthony Parker Jr. on May 17, 1982, he was the first son of Pamela and Tony Parker Sr. A Chicago native, Tony Sr. had been a collegiate basketball star at Loyola who went on to become a star in Europe. An excellent defensive player, Tony Sr. was a member of championship teams in Belgium, France, and the Netherlands. He played for fifteen seasons before going on to become an NBA commentator for French-language television.

Despite his father's basketball prowess, Tony Jr.—who was born in Bruges, Belgium, but raised in France—was initially more interested in soccer than in basketball. But during a 1996 trip to Chicago, Tony, along with his uncle and his two brothers,

Tony Parker races downcourt past New Jersey star Jason Kidd.

visited a Chicago Bulls practice, where they met Scottie Pippen and the legendary Michael Jordan. The unexpected meeting with the NBA stars, coupled with his father's own background on the hardwood, sparked Tony's interest in playing basketball. His goal in the sport was clear: "I want to follow in my father's footsteps, but do it better," he said.[87]

Tony was good enough to be playing professionally by the time he was fifteen years old. He spent two seasons, 1997–1998 and 1998–1999, in the French minor leagues. Parker, who also attended the National Institute for Sports and Physical Education in Paris, played for the French Junior National team in the 1998 European Junior Championships and then signed with Paris Saint-Germain (PSG) in 1999.

He played well as a reserve with PSG, but his breakout moment in the sport did not come with that team. Instead, it came on February 4, 2000. Parker had been chosen to compete at the Nike Hoop Summit, which pitted the best young American players against the best young international stars. During the game, he caught the eye of several university coaches and NBA scouts by scoring twenty points and adding seven assists against a U.S. team that included future NBA star Darius Miles.

Parker decided to stay in France, and in 2000 he once again played with the French Junior National squad. He averaged 25.8 points, 6.8 assists, and 6.8 steals per game, leading France to the championship and taking home MVP honors in the process. He also played thirty games for Paris Basket Racing during the 2000–2001 season, averaging nearly fifteen points and six assists per game. Several colleges, including Georgia Tech and UCLA, were still heavily recruiting Parker. After considering the universities' scholarship offers, Parker opted instead to try his luck in the 2001 NBA draft. "At first, it was like a dream for me, when I was 14, 15," he told Bill Sullivan of the *Sporting News*. "When I was 16, 17, I saw some people getting tryouts for the NBA, and I said, 'Maybe I can do it.'"[88]

Coming to America

Despite Parker's impressive performances in international play, not everyone was familiar with the teenaged point guard. Gregg Popovich, head coach of the San Antonio Spurs, was among those unaware of Parker's abilities—that is, until assistant general manager R.C. Buford tried to convince him to watch a videotape of Parker's performance at the 2000 Nike Hoops Summit during a pre-draft scouting session. "Popovich didn't want to hear about it," wrote Sullivan. "The whole idea seemed absurd."[89]

The coach, who felt that European players rarely made successful transitions to the American style of play, reportedly told Buford, "If he's a three man [a small forward], and he's got

---

NBA commissioner David Stern congratulates Parker after the Spurs had selected him in the first round of the 2001 NBA draft.

a 'vich' at the end of his name, I'll go look at one of my countrymen. But I'm not looking at some French point guard. Give
me a break."[90]

Buford persisted, and finally Popovich agreed to view the
tape. What he saw amazed him—a 6-foot-2, 177-pound point
guard "flashing past defenders into the lane, setting up
teammates for easy shots and playing chest-to-chest defense."[91]

Popovich was convinced. "The more I watched, the more obvious it was," he recalled. "This kid was the real thing."[92]

Popovich wanted to make Parker a Spur. But San Antonio
was not the only NBA team interested in the European star.
The Spurs drafted late in the first round (they had the twenty-
eighth pick), and the chances were good that some other team
would select Parker before San Antonio had an opportunity.
Team after team chose their players, but no one selected a point
guard until Utah took Spain's Raul Lopez with the twenty-
fourth pick. Parker was still available when Vancouver went on
the clock with the twenty-seventh overall pick. Although the
Grizzlies needed a point guard, Vancouver shocked everyone
by taking Iowa State's Jamaal Tinsley instead of Parker.
Popovich would get his man after all. "When he was there,"
the coach said, "we were absolutely stunned."[93]

San Antonio wasted little time selecting Parker with its first-
round pick. Parker was delighted. "It is the team that I wanted
to go to," he said following the draft. "It is one of the top three
teams in the NBA and they have some of the best players, Tim
Duncan and David Robinson. It is going to be so amazing."[94]

The Spurs knew they had acquired a talented basketball
player with a lot of potential. But no one—not Buford,
Popovich, or even Parker himself—could have predicted the
kind of immediate impact he would have on the team.

Wasting Little Time

Coach Popovich and the Spurs' staff appreciated Parker's talent, but they felt that it was a raw talent. At nineteen, Parker
was younger than the average NBA rookie. He had never
played on a U.S. basketball team, and he was not familiar with
the American style of play. On top of that, he would have to ad-

Parker (right) reaches out to steal a pass during a game against Denver. In his first season, Parker averaged 9.2 points and 4.3 assists per game.

just to living in a new country. Popovich assumed it would take time for Parker to find his niche and contribute to the team. Parker had other plans. "He continued to pass tests as easily as he beat defenders off the dribble," reported *Sports Illustrated* writer Phil Taylor. "[Parker] was impressive on the Spurs' summer league team, then in training camp, then coming off the bench in the first few games of the regular season."[95]

Parker had exceeded all expectations, and Popovich decided to put him in the starting lineup after just five regular-season

NBA games. "When the real games started and we saw the same thing, we looked at each other and said, 'What's left? What other hurdle does this guy have to get over before we make this move?'" the coach said.[96] Point guard Antonio Daniels willingly moved over to shooting guard—his natural position—to make room for the French phenom. Parker wasted little time contributing to San Antonio's success. In his first game as a starter, he scored twelve points and added four assists and three rebounds against the Orlando Magic.

Although Parker struggled with his accuracy in his first start, he quickly turned things around. By his second start, a November 8 game against the Charlotte Hornets, he scored twenty-two points and hit four of seven shots from three-point range, prompting Charlotte point guard Baron Davis to say, "Somebody told me he couldn't shoot. Somebody was wrong."[97] Four days later, Parker scored fourteen points and had ten assists against the Detroit Pistons.

In seventy-seven appearances during the 2001–2002 season, Parker averaged 9.2 points, 4.3 assists, 2.6 rebounds, and 1.2 steals per game. He shot 42 percent from the field, 32 percent from three-point range, and 68 percent from the free-throw line. Parker led the Spurs in assists and steals that season. In ten playoff games, he averaged 15.5 points and 4.0 assists. Parker was selected to the NBA All-Rookie First Team, becoming the first foreign-born guard ever to earn the honor, and he had proven that he had what it took to be a force in the league. "It's going to take some time," San Antonio star David Robinson said during Parker's rookie campaign. "But potentially? . . . He's one of the best in the league, potentially."[98]

"On Aime Tony!"

Parker had far surpassed expectations during his first NBA season, and everyone had taken notice. He had begun drawing comparisons with Duncan as a rookie—from his own teammates, no less. "[Parker] doesn't get nervous; he just plays," said Robinson. "The last time I saw a young player who acted like that, it was Tim."[99]

Sports Illustrated writer Phil Taylor agreed with the Admiral's assessment. "Parker's similarity to Duncan . . . is unmistakable," he wrote in a December 2001 article. "Although neither went through the mainstream U.S. sports system, both men play with a wisdom beyond their years. . . . Like Duncan, Parker has an efficient style, free of the bells and whistles that many U.S.-born pros picked up on the playgrounds."[100]

Paris mayor Bertrand Belanoe and Parker hold up promotional T-shirts outside the Paris town hall. Parker is a very popular figure in his native France.

If Parker was beginning to receive a fair amount of acclaim in the United States, in France he was becoming an idol. His sudden rise as one of the NBA's top rookies during the 2001–2002 season turned Parker into a bit of a national obsession. In fact, French fans often attended Spurs home games, exhibiting posters that read "On Aime Tony!"—in English, "We Love Tony!" Parker also started his own website as a rookie, making it available in English and French so that fans on both sides of the Atlantic could follow his career. Many claimed that Tony Parker was the main reason for an increase in the NBA's popularity in France. "He has become a French version of Ichiro Suzuki, the Japanese baseball star who made his countrymen proud with a dazzling rookie season for the Seattle Mariners," claimed Taylor.[101]

Parker's following in Europe surprised just about everyone. French journalist Olivier Pheulpin, who moved to San Antonio solely to cover Parker's exploits, said, "People in France expected nothing of him. We have had other players . . . who have gone to the NBA and done very little, and there was no reason to believe Tony would be different."[102] He was different, however—so much so that Pheulpin wound up doing an interview with the Spurs point guard that filled the front page of *L'Equipe*, the largest sports publication in France. This is an honor rarely granted to an athlete of Parker's age and status. "Tony is very popular for someone who plays a sport that France cares nothing about," Pheulpin observed. "[A front-page interview] usually happens only for soccer players who are World Cup heroes."[103]

From Rookie to Leader

Acclaim notwithstanding, Parker's game was far from perfect during his rookie season. He is small for the NBA and was a sporadic shooter. Some said he also lacked the aggressiveness to play an inside game. However, the main criticism against Parker was that he failed to display the on-court leadership required from a team's point guard.

In his second season, Popovich and the Spurs expected the twenty-year-old guard to take control of games. "Time will tell how mentally tough he is as far as being able to grab a team by the scruff of its neck and impose his will on it," the coach said. "It's a lot to ask of a guy that young. But we have to ask it."[104]

Parker was able to respond. With the Spurs trailing the Dallas Mavericks by sixteen points during a December 11, 2002, game, Parker took over. He scored a career-high thirty-two points that night and led his teammates to a comeback victory. Over the next thirty-seven games Parker averaged 17.8 points per game while hitting on nearly 48 percent of his field goal attempts and more than 78 percent of his free throws. He drove to the basket more and averaged 5.2 attempts from the foul line over that span (more than twice his average during his rookie season). He also became more of a leader. As *San Antonio Express-News* writer Johnny Ludden observed during a March game against Sacramento, there were times when Parker took total control of the game. "Bruce Bowen cut to his right and ran along the baseline. . . . Parker, who had other plans, motioned Bowen back left, looking like a traffic cop directing an overanxious rush-hour driver," Ludden wrote. "When Parker tried to call a play one quarter later, another teammate barked that he wanted something different. 'No,' Parker said, 'we're running this.'"[105] They did run it, much to the delight of Coach Popovich. "Players listen to you when they've come to respect what you've done," he said. "For Tony to finally feel strong enough to do that is a huge, huge step forward."[106]

Parker earned his teammates' respect by playing in every game during the 2002–2003 season, averaging 33.8 minutes of playing time per contest. He improved his scoring to 15.5 points per game in his second year. His assists increased to 5.2 per game, and he improved his shooting percentage across the board, connecting on 46.4 percent of his shots from the field, 33.7 percent from beyond the three-point arc, and 75.5 percent from the penalty stripe. Parker was second on the team in scoring, behind Duncan, and he led San Antonio in assists. On top of that, the Spurs were undefeated in the sixteen games in which Parker scored at least twenty points. Clearly, he was a better all-around player—and one of the main reasons why San Antonio finished with a 60-22 regular-season record. Now he would have to continue to prove his leadership ability—this time, while facing the pressures of playoff elimination.

Stephon Marbury watches as Tony Parker goes to the basket during a 2003 playoff game. Parker had trouble playing against Marbury initially, but the young guard was able to adjust to help the Spurs win the series.

Trial by Fire

Parker and the Spurs met the Phoenix Suns in the first round of the 2002–2003 playoffs, which meant that Parker would be matched up against Stephon Marbury. Marbury had outplayed Parker during the regular season: In six head-to-head meetings, Parker had been limited to 8.3 points and 4.8 assists per game, while hitting just 25 percent of his shots. Marbury had averaged 31.3 points and 7.7 assists during their meetings. Marbury seemed to be able to uncover and exploit Parker's weaknesses better than anyone else in the NBA.

During the first two games of the playoff series, Marbury again had the better of Parker. Parker scored just nine points for the two games combined. He was three-for-twenty from the floor and zero-for-eight from three-point range. Parker missed eleven of thirteen shots in the first game, and he missed a critical free throw late in the game as Phoenix won in overtime. He played only eighteen minutes in game two, sitting for most of the game after getting in early foul trouble. The two points he scored that night were his lowest total since the first game of the 2002–2003 season.

The Suns had completely eliminated Parker as a threat on the court. "Phoenix . . . has done its best to take away Parker's strengths," Ludden wrote following game two. "They have occasionally jumped the Spurs' pick-and-rolls, preventing him from penetrating. When he has gotten into the lane, he's usually had to contend with a shot blocker."[107] Yet somehow, San Antonio managed to win the second game, tying the series at one apiece.

Though the Spurs were still very much alive, they clearly needed their point guard to turn things around. Spurs coach Gregg Popovich decided to try some "tough love" on Parker. After the second game, he challenged Parker to collect himself and play better. "No more babying," the coach said. "I don't care that you're 20. Nobody cares that you're a little bit angry or a little bit embarrassed that you played badly and it's not going your way. Nobody cares. I don't care. The crowd doesn't care. There's not one person on the planet who cares. . . . So figure it out."[108] The message to Parker was clear. He was not a rookie any longer. He was one of San Antonio's impact players, and his team needed him to reach down inside himself and find a way to break out of his slump.

Parker analyzed his play against Marbury and understood what he needed to do. "I learned a lot from the first two games," he said. "I had learned how to approach the game, how to attack. It helped me. I feel more stronger now mentally. I feel more ready to play."[109]

He quickly proved it during game three, hitting an eighteen-footer early in the first quarter and following it up by beating Marbury downcourt for a layup. Parker connected on jump shot after jump shot, adding in a three-pointer for good measure. By the time the buzzer had sounded to end the first quarter, Parker had racked up thirteen points.

He finished the game with twenty-nine points and led San Antonio to a 99-86 victory. His teammates were thrilled, but not necessarily surprised. "Nobody is going to hold Tony down too long," said Robinson. "We knew he was going to come back soon."[110] Added forward Danny Ferry, "The guys on the team believe in him."[111]

Despite being one of the youngest point guards in the league, Tony Parker had proved himself as a leader on the court and in the locker room. He had the unwavering support of the men he played alongside. For a point guard, especially for one as young as Parker, there is no greater honor.

San Antonio Spurs Achievements

Year–by–Year Records

ABA

ABA					PLAYOFFS	
Season	Coach	Finish	W	L	W	L
1967–68	Cliff Hagan	2nd/Western Conf.	46	32	4	4
1968–69	Cliff Hagan	4th/Western Conf.	41	37	3	4
1969–70	Cliff Hagan /Max Williams	2nd/Western Conf.	45	39	2	4
1970–71	Max Williams	4th/Western Conf.	30	54	0	4
1971–72	Tom Nissalke	3rd/Western Conf.	42	42	0	4
1972–73	Babe McCarthy	5th/Western Conf.	28	56	–	–
1973–74	Tom Nissalke	3rd/Western Conf.	45	39	3	4
1974–75	Tom Nissalke /Bob Bass	2nd/Western Conf.	51	33	2	4
1975–76	Bob Bass	3rd/Western Conf.	50	34	3	4

NBA					PLAYOFFS	
Season	Coach	Finish	W	L	W	L
1976–77	Doug Moe	3rd/Central Div.	44	38	0	2
1977–78	Doug Moe	1st/Central Div.	52	30	2	4
1978–79	Doug Moe	1st/Central Div.	48	34	7	7
1979–80	Doug Moe /Bob Bass	2nd/Central Div.	41	41	–	–
1980–81	Stan Albeck	1st/Midwest Div.	52	30	1	2
1981–82	Stan Albeck	1st/Midwest Div.	48	34	3	4
1982–83	Stan Albeck	1st/Midwest Div.	53	29	4	5
1983–84	Morris McHone /Bob Bass	5th/Midwest Div.	37	45	6	5
1984–85	Cotton Fitzsimmons	4th/Midwest Div.	41	41	–	–
1985–86	Cotton Fitzsimmons	6th/Midwest Div.	35	47	2	3
1986–87	Bob Weiss	6th/Midwest Div.	28	54	–	–
1987–88	Bob Weiss	5th/Midwest Div.	31	51	0	3
1988–89	Larry Brown	5th/Midwest Div.	21	61		
1989–90	Larry Brown	1st/Midwest Div.	56	26	6	4

NBA					PLAYOFFS	
Season	Coach	Finish	W	L	W	L
1990–91	Larry Brown	1st/Midwest Div.	55	27	1	3
1991–92	Larry Brown /Bob Bass	2nd/Midwest Div.	47	35	0	3
1992–93	Jerry Tarkanian /John Lucas	2nd/Midwest Div.	49	33	5	5
1993–94	John Lucas	2nd/Midwest Div.	55	27	9	6
1994–95	Bob Hill	1st/Midwest Div.	62	20	9	6
1995–96	Bob Hill	1st/Midwest Div.	59	23	5	5
1996–97	Bob Hill /Gregg Popovich	6th/Midwest Div.	20	62	–	–
1997–98	Gregg Popovich	2nd/Midwest Div.	56	26	4	5
1998–99	Gregg Popovich	1st/Midwest Div.	37	13	15	2
1999–00	Gregg Popovich	2nd/Midwest Div.	53	29	1	3
2000–01	Gregg Popovich	1st/Midwest Div.	58	24	7	6
2001–02	Gregg Popovich	1st Midwest Div.	58	24	4	6
2002–03	Gregg Popovich	1st/Midwest Div.	60	22	16	8

NBA Most Valuable Player (Maurice Podoloff Trophy)

1994–95	David Robinson
2001–02	Tim Duncan
2002–03	Tim Duncan

NBA All-Star Game Most Valuable Player

| 1980 | George Gervin |
| 2000 | Tim Duncan (co-winner) |

NBA Finals Most Valuable Player

| 1999 | Tim Duncan |
| 2003 | Tim Duncan |

ABA Rookie of the Year

| 1973–74 | Swen Nater |

NBA Rookie of the Year (Eddie Gottlieb Trophy)

| 1989–90 | David Robinson |
| 1997–98 | Tim Duncan |

NBA Defensive Player of the Year

| 1985–86 | Alvin Robertson |
| 1991–92 | David Robinson |

NBA Most Improved Player Award

| 1985–86 | Alvin Robertson |

NBA Sportsmanship Award (Joe Dumars Trophy)

1997–98	Avery Johnson
2000–01	David Robinson
2001–02	Steve Smith

Notes

Chapter 1: The Many Faces of Spurs Basketball

1. Quoted in Richard Rambeck, *San Antonio Spurs*. Mankato, MN: Creative Education, 1998, p. 8.
2. Quoted in Dan Zadra, *San Antonio Spurs*. Mankato, MN: Creative Education, 1989, p. 6.
3. Quoted in Zadra, *San Antonio Spurs*, p. 9.
4. Quoted in Zadra, *San Antonio Spurs*, p. 9.
5. Quoted in Zadra, *San Antonio Spurs*, p. 10.
6. Quoted in Arthur Hundhausen, "Remember the ABA: San Antonio Spurs," *Remember the ABA*, 1996. www.geocities.com.
7. Quoted in Rambeck, *San Antonio Spurs*, p. 20.
8. Quoted in Rambeck, *San Antonio Spurs*, p. 21.
9. Quoted in Gene Hoffman, "Spurs History—Twin Tower Power," *SpursCentral.com*, August 2002. www.sahoops.net.
10. Quoted in John Donovan, "The Real MVP," *CNN/Sports Illustrated*, June 26, 1999. http://sportsillustrated.cnn.com.
11. Quoted in Chris Sheridan, "Spurs 88, Nets 77," Associated Press article. *Yahoo! Sports*, June 16, 2003. http://sports.yahoo.com.
12. Quoted in Sheridan, "Spurs 88, Nets 77."

Chapter 2: James Silas

13. Nathan Aaseng, *Comeback Stars of Pro Sports*. Minneapolis, MN: Lerner, 1983, p. 48.
14. Quoted in Dan Pattison, "The Secret Life of James Silas," first published in *Basketball Weekly*, March 1976; reprinted in *Remember the ABA*. www.geocities.com.
15. Quoted in Pattison, "The Secret Life of James Silas."
16. Quoted in Pattison, "The Secret Life of James Silas."
17. Aaseng, *Comeback Stars of Pro Sports*, p. 51.

18. Quoted in John Papanek, "He Surely Is the Spur of the Moment," *Sports Illustrated*, February 5, 1979, p. 20.
19. Quoted in Papanek, "He Surely Is the Spur of the Moment," p. 20.
20. Quoted in Papanek, "He Surely Is the Spur of the Moment," p. 20.
21. Quoted in Papanek, "He Surely Is the Spur of the Moment," p. 21.
22. Quoted in Papanek, "He Surely Is the Spur of the Moment," p. 21.
23. Quoted in Papanek, "He Surely Is the Spur of the Moment," p. 21.
24. Quoted in Papanek, "He Surely Is the Spur of the Moment," p. 21.
25. Quoted in Papanek, "He Surely Is the Spur of the Moment," p. 21.
26. Papanek, "He Surely Is the Spur of the Moment," p. 21.
27. Quoted in Papanek, "He Surely Is the Spur of the Moment," p. 20.

Chapter 3: George Gervin

28. Quoted in NBA Media Ventures, LLC, "NBA History: George Gervin Bio." www.nba.com.
29. Quoted in Zadra, *San Antonio Spurs*, p. 13.
30. John McNamara, *Great Athletes*. Hackensack, NJ: Salem Press/Magill Books, 2001, pp. 843–46.
31. Quoted in Richard O'Connor, "The Lonest Star in Texas," Sport, March 1981, p. 60.
32. Quoted in O'Connor, "The Lonest Star in Texas," p. 60.
33. Quoted in O'Connor, "The Lonest Star in Texas," p. 60.
34. David King, "Iceman Didn't Cometh Too Easily—Owner's Will, Federal Judge Finally Made Gervin a Spur," first published in *San Antonio Express-News*, 1996; reprinted in *Remember the ABA*. www.geocities.com.
35. Quoted in King, "Iceman Didn't Cometh Too Easily."
36. Quoted in Ross Atkin, "Tales of Two Newest Stars in Basketball's Hall of Fame," *Christian Science Monitor*, June 10, 1996, p. 15.
37. Quoted in *AthlonSports.com*, "Athlon's No. 38 NBA Great-

est: George Gervin." www.athlonsports.com.

38. Quoted in Atkin, "Tales of Two Newest Stars in Basketball's Hall of Fame," p. 15.

39. Curry Kirkpatrick, "Iceman Cometh and Scoreth," *Sports Illustrated*, March 6, 1978, p. 15.

40. Quoted in Kirkpatrick, "Iceman Cometh and Scoreth," p. 15.

41. NBA Media Ventures, LLC, "NBA History: George Gervin Bio." www.nba.com.

42. Quoted in Jackie MacMullan, "Two for the Hall," *Sports Illustrated*, May 6, 1996, p. 69.

43. Quoted in O'Connor, "The Lonest Star in Texas," p. 60.

Chapter 4: Johnny Moore

44. Quoted in Neil Rudel, "Johnny Moore: Altoona's First NBA Player Proud to Be a Pioneer," from Blair County Sports Hall of Fame Sixth Induction Awards Dinner program, 1994, p. 8.

45. Quoted in Rudel, "Johnny Moore: Altoona's First NBA Player Proud to Be a Pioneer," p. 9.

46. Quoted in Randy Covitz, "Longhorns' Moore Known for Numbers," *Kansas City Star* website, March 5, 1997. www. kcstar.com.

47. Quoted in Rudel, "Johnny Moore: Altoona's First NBA Player Proud to Be a Pioneer," p. 9.

48. Quoted in Rudel, "Johnny Moore: Altoona's First NBA Player Proud to Be a Pioneer," p. 9.

49. Quoted in Terry Frei, "Moore Is Gunning for Nuggets, Not Moe," *Denver Post*, April 18, 1985, p. 3D.

50. Quoted in Frei, "Moore Is Gunning for Nuggets, Not Moe," p. 3D.

51. Quoted in Frei, "Moore Is Gunning for Nuggets, Not Moe," p. 3D.

52. Quoted in Jim Armstrong, "Brain Surgery Isn't Keeping Moore Down," *Denver Post*, January 24, 1986, p. 6E.

53. Quoted in Armstrong, "Brain Surgery Isn't Keeping Moore Down," p. 6E.

54. Quoted in Armstrong, "Brain Surgery Isn't Keeping Moore Down," p. 6E.

55. Armstrong, "Brain Surgery Isn't Keeping Moore Down," p. 6E.

56. Quoted in Armstrong, "Brain Surgery Isn't Keeping Moore Down," p. 6E.

57. Quoted in Armstrong, "Brain Surgery Isn't Keeping Moore Down," p. 6E.

58. Quoted in Glenn Rogers, "Former Spur Johnny Moore Feels 'Blessed' About His Success," *MySanAntonio.com*, February 2, 2003. www.mysanantonio.com.

59. Quoted in Rogers, "Former Spur Johnny Moore Feels 'Blessed' About His Success."

60. Quoted in Rogers, "Former Spur Johnny Moore Feels 'Blessed' About His Success."

Chapter 5: David Robinson

61. Quoted in Dawn M. Miller, *David Robinson: Backboard Admiral*. Minneapolis, MN: Lerner, 1991, p. 18.

62. Quoted in Miller, *David Robinson: Backboard Admiral*, p. 21.

63. Quoted in John Rolfe, *David Robinson*. Boston: Little, Brown, 1991, p. 27.

64. Quoted in Rolfe, *David Robinson*, p. 33.

65. Quoted in Miller, *David Robinson: Backboard Admiral*, p. 37.

66. Quoted in Miller, *David Robinson: Backboard Admiral*, p. 10.

67. Quoted in Rolfe, *David Robinson*, p. 113.

68. Quoted in Ken Rappoport, *Tim Duncan: Star Forward*. Berkeley Heights, NJ: Enslow, 2000, p. 94.

69. Craig Daniels, "David Robinson's Vindication," *SLAM! Basketball*, June 26, 1999. www.canoe.ca.

70. David Robinson with Phil Taylor, "Mission Accomplished," *CNN/Sports Illustrated*, July 13, 1999. http://sportsillus trated.cnn.com.

71. Quoted in Johnny Ludden, "Robinson's Not Looking Back Yet," *MySanAntonio.com*, October 27, 2002. www.mysanan tonio.com.

72. Quoted in Johnny Ludden, "Spurs Notebook: Rivers Calls Robinson the Ashe of Basketball," *MySanAntonio.com*, February 1, 2003. www.mysanantonio.com.

Chapter 6: Tim Duncan

73. Quoted in *Current Biography*. Bronx, NY: H.W. Wilson, 1999. Accessed online at http://vnweb.hwwilsonweb.com.
74. Quoted in Rappoport, *Tim Duncan: Star Forward*, p. 23–24.
75. Quoted in Rappoport, *Tim Duncan: Star Forward*, p. 36–37.
76. Quoted in Rappoport, *Tim Duncan: Star Forward*, p. 83.
77. Quoted in Rappoport, *Tim Duncan: Star Forward*, p. 91.
78. Quoted in Rappoport, *Tim Duncan: Star Forward*, p. 10.
79. Quoted in Rappoport, *Tim Duncan: Star Forward*, p. 11.
80. Quoted in "Duncan: A Quiet, Boring, Dominant MVP," *CNN/Sports Illustrated*, June 28, 1999. http://sportsillustrated.cnn.com.
81. Quoted in "Duncan: A Quiet, Boring, Dominant MVP."
82. Quoted in David DuPree, "Duncan the Quiet Giant of the NBA," *USA Today*, January 29, 2003, p. 1c.
83. Quoted in "Duncan: A Quiet, Boring, Dominant MVP."
84. Quoted in DuPree, "Duncan the Quiet Giant of the NBA."
85. DuPree, "Duncan the Quiet Giant of the NBA."
86. Quoted in DuPree, "Duncan the Quiet Giant of the NBA."

Chapter 7: Tony Parker

87. Quoted in "A Family Thing," from Tony Parker's official website. www.tonyparker.net.
88. Quoted in Bill Sullivan, "Foreign Influence," *Sporting News*, December 24, 2001, pp. 34–36.
89. Sullivan, "Foreign Influence," pp. 34-36.
90. Quoted in Sullivan, "Foreign Influence," pp. 34–36.
91. Phil Taylor, "Avant-Guard," *Sports Illustrated*, December 12, 2001, pp. 74–77.
92. Quoted in Taylor, "Avant-Guard," pp. 74–77.
93. Quoted in Sullivan, "Foreign Influence," pp. 34–36.
94. Quoted in "From Dream to Reality," from Tony Parker's official website. www.tonyparker.net.
95. Taylor, "Avant-Guard," pp. 74–77.
96. Quoted in Sullivan, "Foreign Influence," pp. 34–36.
97. Quoted in Taylor, "Avant-Guard," pp. 74–77.
98. Quoted in Sullivan, "Foreign Influence," pp. 34–36.
99. Quoted in Taylor, "Avant-Guard," pp. 74–77.

100. Taylor, "Avant-Guard," pp. 74–77.
101. Taylor, "Avant-Guard," pp. 74–77.
102. Quoted in Taylor, "Avant-Guard," pp. 74–77.
103. Quoted in Taylor, "Avant-Guard," pp. 74–77.
104. Quoted in Johnny Ludden, "Point Man Tony Parker's Breakout Season a Big Reason for San Antonio's Surge in the Standings," *MySanAntonio.com*, March 4, 2003. www.mysanantonio.com.
105. Ludden, "Point Man Tony Parker's Breakout Season a Big Reason for San Antonio's Surge in the Standings."
106. Quoted in Ludden, "Point Man Tony Parker's Breakout Season a Big Reason for San Antonio's Surge in the Standings."
107. Johnny Ludden, "Parker Struggling Against Suns' Marbury," *MySanAntonio.com*, April 23, 2003. www.mysanantonio.com.
108. Quoted in Johnny Ludden, "Spurs' Young Guys Give Team Playoff Lift," *MySanAntonio.com*, May 3, 2003. www.mysanantonio.com.
109. Quoted in Johnny Ludden, "Parker Leads Spurs to Win over Phoenix with 29 Points," *MySanAntonio.com*, April 26, 2003. www.mysanantonio.com.
110. Quoted in Ludden, "Parker Leads Spurs to Win over Phoenix with 29 Points."
111. Quoted in Ludden, "Parker Leads Spurs to Win over Phoenix with 29 Points."

For Further Reading

Hal Bock, *David Robinson*. Philadelphia: Chelsea House, 1997. A brief biography that looks at the legendary center's rise to stardom.

Aaron Frisch, *The History of the San Antonio Spurs*. Mankato, MN: The Creative Company, 2002. Photo-heavy profiles of Alvin Robertson, Swen Nater, Larry Kenon, and other stars from the Spurs' past and present.

Jan Hubbard, ed., *One for San Antonio: The 1999 Official NBA Finals Retrospective*. New York: Random House Trade Paperbacks, 1999. The NBA's official tribute to the Spurs' 1999 championship team. Features more than 150 photos.

Paul Joseph, *Inside the NBA: San Antonio Spurs*. Minneapolis, MN: Abdo & Daughters, 1997. Covers the history and personalities of a team that missed the playoffs only four times in its first 26 years.

Ambrose Robinson, et al., *How to Raise an MVP*. Grand Rapids, MI: Zondervan, 1996. The parents of Spurs center David Robinson discuss how they raised their famous son.

Jim Savage, *The Force: David Robinson*. New York: Dell, 1992. An examination of Robinson's professional career and personal life.

Stew Thornley, *Sports Super Star Tim Duncan*. Berkeley Heights, NJ: Enslow, 2001. A basic biography chronicling Duncan's life from his childhood in St. Croix through his 1999–2000 season with San Antonio.

Works Consulted

Books

Nathan Aaseng, *Comeback Stars of Pro Sports*. Minneapolis, MN: Lerner, 1983.

Current Biography. Bronx, NY: H.W. Wilson, 1999. A collection of biographies, published in magazine and yearbook formats.

John McNamara, *Great Athletes*. Hackensack, NJ: Salem Press/Magill Books, 2001. Profiles of sports superstars.

Dawn M. Miller, *David Robinson: Backboard Admiral*. Minneapolis, MN: Lerner, 1991. Examines the college and professional career of the Navy grad and San Antonio star.

Richard Rambeck, *San Antonio Spurs*. Mankato, MN: Creative Education, 1998. Describes the background and history of the Spurs franchise through 1997.

Ken Rappoport, *Tim Duncan: Star Forward*. Berkeley Heights, NJ: Enslow, 2000. Discusses the personal life and professional career of the basketball star from the Virgin Islands.

John Rolfe, *David Robinson*. Boston: Little, Brown, 1991. A *Sports Illustrated for Kids* book that provides a surprisingly deep and informative look at the Admiral's life and career.

Dan Zadra. *San Antonio Spurs*. Mankato, MN: Creative Education, 1989. A brief history of the San Antonio club from its beginning through the signing of David Robinson in 1988.

Periodicals

Jim Armstrong, "Brain Surgery Isn't Keeping Moore Down," *Denver Post*, January 24, 1986, p. 6E.

Ross Atkin, "Tales of Two Newest Stars in Basketball's Hall of Fame," *Christian Science Monitor*, June 10, 1996, p. 15.

David DuPree, "Duncan the Quiet Giant of the NBA," *USA To-*

day, January 29, 2003, p. 1c.

Terry Frei, "Moore Is Gunning for Nuggets, Not Moe," *Denver Post*, April 18, 1985, p. 3D.

Curry Kirkpatrick, "Iceman Cometh and Scoreth," *Sports Illustrated*, March 6, 1978, p. 15.

Jackie MacMullan, "Two for the Hall," *Sports Illustrated*, May 6, 1996, p. 69.

Richard O'Connor, "The Lonest Star in Texas," *Sport*, March 1981, p. 60.

John Papanek, "He Surely Is the Spur of the Moment," *Sports Illustrated*, February 5, 1979, p. 20.

Neil Rudel, "Johnny Moore: Altoona's First NBA Player Proud to Be a Pioneer," from Blair County Sports Hall of Fame Sixth Induction Awards Dinner program, 1994, p. 8.

Bill Sullivan, "Foreign Influence," *Sporting News*, December 24, 2001, pp. 34–36.

Phil Taylor, "Avant-Guard," *Sports Illustrated*, December 12, 2001, pp. 74–77.

Internet Sources

AthlonSports.com, "Athlon's No. 38 NBA Greatest: George Gervin." www.athlonsports.com.

Michael Bonner and Gene Hoffman, "Spurs History—The Admiral Arrives," *SpursCentral.com*, August 2002. www.sahoops.net.

Randy Covitz, "Longhorns' Moore Known for Numbers," *Kansas City Star* website, March 5, 1997. www.kcstar.com.

Craig Daniels, "David Robinson's vindication," SLAM! Basketball, June 26, 1999. www.canoe.ca.

John Donovan, "The Real MVP," CNN/*Sports Illustrated*, June 26, 1999. http://sportsillustrated.cnn.com.

"Duncan: A Quiet, Boring, Dominant MVP," *CNN/Sports Illustrated*, June 28, 1999. http://sportsillustrated.cnn.com.

Gene Hoffman, "Spurs History—Twin Tower Power," *SpursCentral.com*, August 2002. www.sahoops.net.

Arthur Hundhausen, "Remember the ABA: San Antonio Spurs," *Remember the ABA*, 1996. www.geocities.com.

David King, "Iceman Didn't Cometh Too Easily—Owner's Will, Federal Judge Finally Made Gervin a Spur," first published in *San Antonio Express-News*, 1996; reprinted in *Remember the ABA*. www.geocities.com.

Johnny Ludden, "Parker Leads Spurs to Win over Phoenix with 29 Points," *MySanAntonio.com*, April 26, 2003. www.mysanantonio.com.

_____, "Parker Struggling Against Suns' Marbury," *MySanAntonio.com*, April 23, 2003. www.mysanantonio.com.

_____, "Point Man Tony Parker's Breakout Season a Big Reason for San Antonio's Surge in the Standings," *MySanAntonio.com*, March 4, 2003. www.mysanantonio.com.

_____, "Robinson's not Looking Back Yet," *MySanAntonio.com*, October 27, 2002. www.mysanantonio.com.

_____, "Spurs Notebook: Rivers Calls Robinson the Ashe of Basketball," *MySanAntonio.com*, February 1, 2003. www.mysanantonio.com.

_____, "Spurs' Young Guys Give Team Playoff Lift," *MySanAntonio.com*, May 3, 2003. www.mysanantonio.com.

NBA Media Ventures, LLC, "NBA History: George Gervin Bio." www.nba.com.

———, "San Antonio Spurs History," NBA.com, 2003. www.nba.com.

Dan Pattison, "The Secret Life of James Silas," first published in *Basketball Weekly*, March 1976; reprinted in *Remember the ABA*. www.geocities.com.

David Robinson with Phil Taylor, "Mission Accomplished," *CNN/Sports Illustrated*, July 13, 1999. http://sportsillustrated.cnn.com.

Glenn Rogers, "Former Spur Johnny Moore Feels 'Blessed' About His Success," *MySanAntonio.com*, February 2, 2003. www.mysanantonio.com.

Chris Sheridan, "Spurs 88, Nets 77," Associated Press article. Yahoo! Sports. June 16, 2003. http://sports.yahoo.com.

Websites

Tim Duncan (www.slamduncan.com). This is the official website of the 2001–2002 and 2001–2003 NBA Most Valuable Player.

Tony Parker (www.tonyparker.net). This is the official website of San Antonio's French-raised point guard.

San Antonio Spurs (www.nba.com/spurs). This is the team's official website. It includes news, statistics, history, and more and is accessible through NBA.com.

Index

Picture Credits

Cover photo: AP/Wide World Photos
© AP/Wild World Photos, 21, 42, 45, 62, 68, 73, 78, 85, 87, 92
© Bettmann/Corbis, 55, 60
© Mike Blake/Reuters/Landov, 7, 71, 80
© Paul Buck/EPA/Landov, 83
© Xavier L'Hospice/Reuters/Landov, 89
© Jeff Mitchell/Reuters/Landov, 75
© NBAE/Getty Images, 52
© Photofest, 16, 51
© Remember the ABA, 9, 11, 12, 13, 28, 30, 33, 34, 37, 39
© Reuters/Landov, 19, 24, 77
© Mike Segar/Reuters/Landov, 58
© Stephen F. Austin State University, 26, 27
© Ray Stubblebine/Reuters/Landov, 66
© University of Texas Athletic Department, 47, 48

About the Author

Chuck Bednar is a freelance writer and editor from Win-
tersville, Ohio. He was born in 1976 and holds an Associate of
Arts degree in journalism from Jefferson Community College.
Bednar started as a staff sports reporter with newspapers in
Ohio and West Virginia. Since then, he has served as a baseball
editor, business columnist, book reviewer, trivia writer, and
other positions. This is his fifth sports-related book.